Devoted to Antiquing

Tammy Hinton

Denton, Texas

Dedication

This book is dedicated to the Robert M. Thorn family of Pennsylvania, and the Phipps family of Oklahoma. Although the Phipps are all deceased, I know they rest in heavenly peace in the arms of our Father.

And the McSherry Writers Guild of McAlester, Oklahoma, who mentored me for the last five years.

And my wonderful husband, Herb Hinton.

Scripture quotations are taken from the Authorized (King James) Version of the Bible.

Devoted Books
An imprint of AWOC.COM Publishing
P.O. Box 2819
Denton, TX 76202

© 2012 by Tammy Hinton
All Rights Reserved.

No part of this publication may be reproduced, stored in a retrieval system, or transmitted in any form or by any means, electronic, mechanical, recording or otherwise, without written permission, except in the case of brief quotations embodied in critical articles and reviews.

Manufactured in the United States of America

ISBN: 978-1-62016-008-4

Table of Contents

Foreword 5
Mr. President 8
Mother of Our Country's China 11
Sad Eyes Peer Back 15
The Free Bookcase 18
The Rattan Chair 25
A Penny for Your Thoughts 33
Mi Familia, My Family 37
Look for the Silver Lining 42
Three Generations of Noritake 47
Give Me a Hug 49
Occupied Japan 52
A Real Cup of Tea 55
The Innocence of a Child 58
As Time Goes By 61
Cut Glass or Pressed That Is the Question 65
There Is Beauty in the Midst of Despair 69
The Potter's Hands 72
Grandma's Gift 76
You're A Doll 80
Yes, I Can 88
Don't Fence Me In 93
It Pays to Advertise 96
It Pays to Advertise–Part II 102
A Stitch in Time 108
Uncle Sam Needs You–Bob[3] 112
Bibliography 118

Foreword

Webster's Pocket Dictionary defines the word antique as "An object, esp. a work of art, or handicraft, valued because of its age."

"Collector—a person who collects books, paintings, stamps, shells, etc., especially as a hobby." Dictionary.com.

When I started collecting, the standard was it had to be 100 years old or older to be considered an antique. Along the way the benchmark changed to fifty, and in today's market the waters are still murkier as collectables vie with antiques. Even in our cash short economy, baby boomers continue to buy that special toy or record that they had when they were a kid. Their children have become collectors at an earlier age then their parents. A quick visit to any self-respecting antique store contains a supply of Star Wars and Barbie memorabilia for the Generation X collectors.

For both collectors and retailers, individual television shows such as PBS's highest rated series, Antiques Roadshow, and the History Channel's American Pickers, are both a blessing and a curse depending on which side of the table you are standing on.

Until recently, my mom was an antique dealer in Bucks County, Pennsylvania for over forty years. She provided stock to retailers and set up at flea markets by attending auctions and estate sales. Three floors of her house, which was built in 1737, her barn, milk house, and garages bulged with both trash and treasures. Assisted by the men in our family, she maneuvered many an armoire, cabinet, or oak bookcase up and down flights of stairs, and to and from her old van. One July I asked her in jest, as I was poring sweat, if she could please buy attics in the winter and basements in the summer. I already knew the answer. You bought when the opportunity presented itself.

For me, whether I had to get up at 3 a.m. to be on the road and setup at a flea market, or browsing in her barn each day, being her lackey (that's another term for unpaid help), was a history lesson. While she may have been running numbers in her brain on what she should offer for the lot or how much she could make, I was picturing the time period of the item and its use.

We shared some years of challenges, but we really bonded on these excursions. Mother and I were able to be peers in our quest for that elusive Tiffany lamp or Chippendale chair. God showed us a way to a devoted mother/daughter relationship. Once again we walk the road of Christian love. I am so blessed. I hope the reader experiences God's love like I have.

When Mom decided to retire and downsize we kids were thrilled. None of us wanted to be responsible to organize her sale. I flew to Pennsylvania from Oklahoma and packed for days to get her ready. On their pre-event walk through, the auctioneers were amazed to find how much she had accumulated over the years. The auction house owner told me he didn't do home sales anymore, "because people won't attend and money is tight." He only booked Mom's because they had been friends for such a long time. To both our amazement, instead of one sale they held three.

This book is for the average collector and describes items that you may realistically find in a mid-American setting. Pricing is in a constant flux. I suggest you invest in the latest version of *Kovels' Antique and Collectables Price List*, *Warman's*, or a resource aimed at the particular item you are seeking. Checking the internet is a good idea before you go shopping for a "find." If you're not a collector, I hope the contents of this book becomes a companion to your favorite TV show and provides some history of the period, along with a chuckle or two.

I hope you enjoy this journey and experience how our Father's teachings can influence our daily lives, learn some historical trivia, terminology, and get some hints you can use.

Let's go.

Mr. President

There is that maketh himself rich, yet hath nothing; there is that maketh himself poor, yet hath great riches.

Proverbs 13:7

Any book dealing in part on American history needs to begin with a story about our Presidents.

We were lined up along the street outside the red brick building waiting. Everyone in our elementary school carried a flag to wave when the signal was given. Since there were a hundred eight year-old boys in the group, some of the flags were weapons of choice to pass the time until we could see his car. It seemed an eternity until the convertible carrying the President turned the corner. I'll never forget him smiling and waving his hat. President Dwight David Eisenhower was an American hero.

George Washington wore the first political button. Since there was no real campaign it was a button to celebrate his becoming President. He and his supporters sported a brass or flat copper clothing button imprinted with "G.W." in the middle and "Long Live the President" around the top. Since it was designed to function as a clothing button, it required being sewn onto the lapel. A second version hung as a pendant on a string. There were about twenty-seven designs to commemorate the event. They average between $1500 and $5000 in today's market.

Andrew Jackson's unsuccessful bid for the Presidency in 1824 introduced the medalets. These were coin sized, less than an inch and three quarters, and coin shaped metal tokens with the candidates likeness imprinted on them. The token contained a hole in the top so it could be worn as a necklace, or attached to a ribbon or string.

Ribbons appeared in the 1800 election. Besides being pinned to a garment, they were used as bookmarks. Usually, they were made of silk. After the Civil War fringe and tassels adorned them thus the name, ribbon badges. By the end of the century they came with pins or clasps and were popular with delegates attending political conventions.

Ferrotype (photos on metal) of candidates encased in metal frames followed. Collectors refer to this type of button as a shell badge. They may have paper photographs of the politician instead of a ferrotype. Lincoln's 1860 campaign button is a sought after treasure by serious collectors. A beardless Lincoln is on the front face and his choice for vice president, Hannibal Hamlin, is on the reverse side. One sold on ebay.com recently for over a thousand dollars.

The Golden Age of campaign buttons (1896-1916) started with the hotly contested presidential race between William McKinley and William Jennings Bryan. McKinley was the last President in the 19th Century and the first one in the 20th Century. Whitehead & Hoag of New Jersey received a patent in July of 1896 for a celluloid button with a metal pin attached to the back to fasten the button to a lapel. They inserted a piece of paper in the back with advertising for their firm. These are referred to as "back papers." Early examples show a round metal disk covered with a printed paper and sealed with a thin piece of celluloid, which is regarded as the first thermoplastic. The likeness of the candidate was printed on a piece of paper, sealed in a thin piece of celluloid, wrapped over a metal button, and secured with a metal ring or "collet" pressed into the back. Pictures, slogans, and bright colors added to the public's demand for the small tokens. This Golden Age provided the most beautiful and ornate buttons; the ones the collectors are on the lookout for to complete their displays.

Lithograph buttons came into vogue during the Woodrow Wilson era. The image was printed onto a piece of tin, stamped out, and adorned with a pin. The lack of a protective layer left lithographed buttons more likely to get scratched and damaged.

Of course collectors want the button that is in pristine condition, rarest, and/or the most clever. A Washington, Lincoln, or John F. Kennedy, can command a high price. A "Cox for President" button from 1920 sold for $100,000. A photo of Cox and his little known vice president, FDR, grace the prize pin.

Franklin Roosevelt became President at a critical time in our history. The Great Depression followed by another World War called for a President with optimism and leadership. The charismatic FDR was the spark that ignited the national spirit. His decision to run for a third term broke with the tradition set by George Washington of serving only two terms. Many pins of the time reflect both positive "Two Good Terms Deserve Another" and negative "No Third Term" slogans. After FDR's death, Congress made two terms the legal limit making him the only man in history to serve three terms.

Buttons that show both the Presidential and Vice Presidential nominees are called jugates. Pins that also endorse state or local candidates are referred to as coattails. Many reproductions have been manufactured. Both The American Oil Company and the Kleenex Company had sets made as giveaways in the 1960s and 1970s.  Fakes will have an inscription on the inner edge on the back, the curl, showing it is a reproduction. Buttons should be kept out of direct light to keep them from fading.

Many twentieth century buttons of national, state, and local contests are collectable. Cultural movements such as women's suffrage, civil rights, and prohibition are also in demand. The choices are so broad that many collectors narrow their collections to a period of time, party affiliation, type of lapel device, etc. Buttons vary in price allowing anyone to start a collection.

Thank you for bringing the people we need in times of desperation. Their leadership keeps this "one Nation under God" on the course set by our fore-fathers when the United States was founded. Each generation is met by new challenges. Help us meet them with dignity, honor, and Godliness.

Trivia: Dirty politics is not a product of recent campaigns. In the race for the Presidency in 1884 Grover Cleveland's opponent, James Blaine, made public that Cleveland had fathered an out of wedlock child in 1874. "Ma, Ma where's my Pa?" became their rallying cry. Blaine later stated he believed he lost the election not because of his policies, but because of a backlash to this tactic. Cleveland supporters countered their victory with, "Gone to the White House, Ha, Ha, Ha!"

Mother of Our Country's China

Judge not, and ye shall not be judged: condemn not and ye shall not be condemned: forgive, and ye shall be forgiven.   Luke 6:37

Each time I go to Independence Hall in Philadelphia I'm in awe of what transpired during Revolutionary times in Franklin's "City of Brotherly Love." Within walking distance of the Hall you can visit Betsey Ross's house, a United States Mint, and most exciting for me, Christ Church located at 20 North American Street.

Established in 1695 as the first Church of England (Anglican) parish in Quaker Pennsylvania, the graveyard contains such notables as Ben Franklin and his wife, Deborah, and four signers of the Declaration of Independence.

It was the sanctuary that held the biggest personal thrill for me. I sat on the pew that belonged to George and Martha Washington. Yes, on a cushion in a white wooden reserved-box, in the three hundred year old church, where the first President of the United States of America and his First Lady sat and worshiped our Lord. I still get excited to think about being in the presence of our Savior and the memory of the most dynamic figure in the founding of our nation.

Little is written of the original First Lady of the United States of America, Martha "Patsy" Dandridge Custis Washington. Martha Dandridge was born on Chestnut Grove Plantation in Virginia in 1731. Women of her day were taught their job was to serve in the advancement of their spouse. They were educated to read and write as tools to keep the household functioning so their husbands need not worry as they focused on their own interests.

At age eighteen young Martha married a wealthy neighbor, Daniel Parke Custis, who was twenty years her senior. The newlyweds resided at his home known as the White House Plantation. In the next seven years before his sudden death, the couple had four children. Two children died in early childhood. One son, John, and one daughter, Martha, lived to be adults.

In 1757 Martha Custis was a wealthy young widow with a drove of suitors. Her wealth allowed her the choice of a husband based on her own desires not the need to be "taken care of." The very private Martha wanted a husband who could make interesting conversation and was a gentleman. She found both qualities in a young planter, militia officer, and future politician by the name of George Washington. They married on January 6, 1759, and Martha and her son and daughter took up residence with him at Mount Vernon.

It is speculated that George Washington could not father children because of a bout of small pox he suffered in his youth or from the mercury oxide used to treat small pox and malaria during that period. However, he assumed the role of their step-father with ease. Unfortunately, Martha's daughter, Martha, died when she was 17 years old during an epileptic seizure. The couple's son, John Custis, served as an aide to the General during the War for Independence and died at age 27 from typhus. John left two children, who were raised by George and Martha Washington.

At the end of the war Martha's idyllic wish for them to retire to Mount Vernon and live the quiet country life was short lived. Urged by friends to attend the Constitutional Convention in 1787, Philadelphia became their home again. In 1789 the Electoral College unanimously elected George Washington the first President of the United States. George coined the phrase "Mister President" when addressed. There was no title "First Lady" so Martha was called "Lady" Washington.

Although Martha felt her new role was limiting and demanding, she realized her actions would define the responsibilities of future First Ladies. Her home was the nation's home, open to local and foreign dignitaries at will. She would have no private life while in office.

At the end of George's second term in December of 1797, the couple took up residence at Mount Vernon. George died on December 14, 1799. Martha outlived her husband by two years, dying at the age of 70 on May 22, 1802.

One of the grandchildren Martha and George raised, George Washington Parke Custis, built a house on the land he inherited in Arlington, Virginia in 1802. He fathered four children, but only one daughter survived to be an adult, Mary Anna Randolph Custis.

Many pieces of Martha Washington's white and cornflower designed china finally went to her great-granddaughter Mary. Young Mary Custis married a gallant soldier, a graduate of West Point, Lieutenant Robert E. Lee in the parlor of her family home, Arlington House. During the Civil War, General and Mrs. Lee's home and contents were confiscated. Arlington House's land became Arlington National Cemetery. The porcelain and china became the property of the Federal Patent Office. Public sentiment against the Lee family kept the articles in limbo until President McKinley returned them in 1901.

You may view examples of porcelain on the National Parks Service U. S. Dept. of the Interior, Arlington House website:

www.nps.gov/muesum/exhibits/arho

Pictured at the left is a piece of the breakfast set by Mottahedeh used by George and Martha Washington. The china was produced in Canton, China and arrived on the first American ship entered in the China Trade. Referred to as the Society of Cincinnati set, because of the Society's emblem in the center, it was presented to him as the first President General of the organization. It is on display at Arlington House.

Needless to say items from the Washington family are priceless and are held in museums. Over the last two hundred years many items have been produced in honor of the couple. Everything from plates containing their portraits to a reproduction of Martha's shoes can be found at a reasonable price.

Lead me in my quest to preserve our history so that future generations can understand the significance of our ancestors thirst for freedom. The most precious freedom being our First Amendment Right: Congress shall make no law respecting an establishment of religion, or prohibiting the free exercise thereof; or abridging the freedom of speech, or of the press; or the right of the people peaceably to assemble, and to petition the Government for a redress of grievances.

> **Hint**: If you plan to travel to Philadelphia to visit Independence Hall you will need to secure tickets. Tickets are free and will assign you a time to tour the site. More information is available at:
>
> http://www.nps.gov/inde
>
> or http://www.independencevisitorcenter.com
>
> or call Independence Visitor Center - 215-965-2305.

Sad Eyes Peer Back

To him that over-cometh will I give to eat of the tree of life, which is in the midst of the paradise of God.

Revelation 2:7

My grandmother was from a family of Methodist ministers and kept the faith even in times of turmoil and confusion in her life. When she was six months old, her young mother died nursing the sick during an epidemic. My great-grandfather took the train back to Ohio and left my grandmother and her sister with his in-laws.

Letters in my possession reflect a lonely child imploring her father to write and visit more. He didn't. He relocated to Pennsylvania and remarried. His new wife and he had a second family. He never returned for the girls.

Her maternal grandparents raised her and her sister, Grace, in an extended family on their farm in Ohio. Sad eyes peer back from photos taken during her childhood. What was she thinking? Did she feel abandoned? Did she wonder why her father didn't love her?

She never judged him. She never withheld her love as punishment for his lack of attention. Her love was boundless. As a true Christian would, she was there for him when he died at age ninety-three. God said honor your mother and father. She never questioned our Lord's word.

When I started doing the family genealogy fifteen years ago, I made it a goal to find the names of all the twenty-two people in the photograph with my grandmother. She is about eight or ten years old so I knew it was taken at her grandparents in Ohio.

It took me about ten years of research to determine everyone's name. It's funny how you build a relationship with people you have never met. Suddenly, you feel you know them. You know their likes and dislikes. Although, it's more likely your perceptions are wrong. Still, through my research I found that my great-great-grandfather bred Percheron draft horses. In the photo he is showing the animal for the photographer as if he were competing in the Ohio State Fair. If pride be a sin, this man is brimming over with transgressions. What I, his grand-daughter, choose to see is a man with unrelenting love for both men and animals. Grandpa Neptune was a man who provided food and shelter to four generations of his family, including his mother-in-law. He was a true man of God.

How many times do we get pictures back and never make a note of the date or who is in the picture for future reference. Okay, scrap bookers do. Anyone else?

Pictures as we know them date back to the Civil War. The wet plate process required a rolling dark room of chemicals to dry glass plate negatives. In 1885 George Eastman developed a wet plate film at the same time American and European companies invented lighter weight, less cumbersome cameras. Eastman introduced the world to film on rolls to make photography available to everyone.

Vintage print: A positive image that has been developed by the photographer from the original negative at the time the picture is taken.

Non-vintage print: A print made at a later date from the negative. Reprints can usually be identified.

Original prints may start at just a few dollars depending on the subject and period of the photo. Civil War period photos start higher as the time period and historical value are factors. The terms "antique" and "vintage" means you are going to pay more for the item. Frames can also add to the value of the piece. A bubble glass frame may have kept the encased photo from being damaged and helped determine age, but please be aware that bubble glass frames can also be reproductions.

Let me be a blessing in the lives of others. My transgressions were forgiven. I am loved. May I lead others to Your Grace. Thank you for providing us with those people in our life who model the principles of a true Christian. May I walk in their footsteps and exhibit those principles in each day of my life.

> **Trivia**: George Eastman and his mother made up the word Kodak for his simple roll film cameras. They used an anagram set. George Eastman was creating his own publicity and decided the name should be short, pronounceable, and not associated with anything else but his product. Kodak caught on with the public, so he added it permanently to the company name.

The Free Bookcase

The generous soul shall be enriched, and he that gives water shall be watered himself.   Proverbs 11:25

In 1976, I traveled from Louisiana to visit my folks and go to the bicentennial celebration in Philadelphia. At the time Mom was an antique dealer in Bucks County, Pennsylvania. As I cruised through her out buildings, I noticed an old three door bookcase stored in the back of her garage. She'd bought it as part of a household, and hated it because of its deep red cherry stain used in the Victorian period. So there it had set for several months in a dark corner never seeing light except when she moved her van. What a waste. She saw me check it out and said, "If you want it take it." Before she could change her mind, I loaded that bookcase in a U-Haul trailer and pulled it a thousand miles home.

Now, every good antique furniture dealer or appraiser will tell you not to refinish antique furniture. And they are correct. You mess with the patina, etc. and you'll devalue the resale price of the item. Don't refinish unless you have a piece that you intend to use yourself rather than resale.

Once back home I laid out some newspaper in my carport, removed one shelf from the bookcase, and applied EZ Strip according to directions. Oh my goodness! It couldn't be - tiger oak. The entire bookcase was tiger oak. Yep, under that awful cherry stain it was oak. When stripped, wiped down, and polished with beeswax, it was beautiful. Since then it has stood as the centerpiece of my living room. Mom kicks herself every time she sees it.

Most vintage collectors want furniture made from oak, walnut, and mahogany. They may seek out a certain design period, furniture maker, or material used. Brass hardware should be from the time period. There are flea market vendors that sell vintage hardware. You can re-do broken parts, but it will de-value the piece. Don't try to buff out scratches and wear as that helps authenticate its age.

Attics are a wonderful place to search for antique furniture; especially if the attic belongs to a generous friend or relative. You then have a piece to remember them by and usually the price is reasonable.

Estate sales offer an opportunity to find an old cared for piece. Household auctions are another good resource. Go before the sale and inspect each item before you bid. Visit antique stores and see what that grandfather clock is going for before you pay too much. Look at authentic pieces so you can spot a reproduction. Most importantly, don't buy on impulse. Be well informed about what to look for and what you should pay.

I'm sorry, but it's hard for me to walk through furniture stores and see the exorbitant prices paid for the poor quality of furniture produced today. Cheap veneer and particle board have replaced solid wood construction and beautiful craftsmanship.

I've been offered $6,000.00 for my free bookcase. It's not for sale. It'll be passed on to my daughter. Fine furniture is like that.

Only God can create the beauty we see in nature every day. Let me take the time to look at the patina in wood, the colors of the trees as summer turns to fall, or the breath taking beauty of the sun rising each morning. Guide us on the best use of our environment. Decisions made today will affect generations.

Trivia: Napoleon Bonaparte understood the use of symbols to convey his power. He used the architectural designs of the Greek, Roman, and Egyptian empires, plus bold colors and gilding in buildings and furniture to inspire his citizens to support his age of conquest. The Emperor supported arts that proclaimed France as the "New Rome." Today we would call that good marketing.

Terminology:

- **Art Deco, 1920s-1930s:** Coined at the 1925 Exposition Internationale des Arts Decoratifs Industriels et Modernes, held in Paris, the heart of the movement existed in America. The style embraced the machine age with its sleek stylized motifs. Art Deco created furniture with brash geometric lines.
- **Art Nouvea, 1896-1914:** French for "new art." "Art for art's sake" was the theme of the period. A style that was popular in Europe and America in the 1890s as a repudiation of Victorian. Also referred to as "Whiplash" because of the undulating sensuous curves employed by Art Nouveua artisans. Legs bow gracefully instead of the straight lines of the past. The lines were simpler and contained more relaxed organic themes.
- **Art Furniture, 1880-1914:** There were no rules. Buyers saw wide use of turned moldings, dark woods, and bamboo to produce a fluid movement. Legs were inclined to be straight. Feet were small.
- **Arts and Craft Movement, 1860-1939:** The Movement started as a protest for the poor quality of goods produced since the start of the Industrial Revolution. It was defined by the high quality of the material used and the craftsmanship employed. The Mission Style, associated with the Franciscan missions of California, was a prime example. The lines of the design were straight and the wood of choice was oak. Furniture maker Gustav Stickley was a noted craftsman.
- **Baroque, 1600s-1700s:** French word for odd. A European style taken from late Roman Catholic churches and palaces of the 1700s. Built to impress, Baroque was greatly ornamented with angels, cherubs, nymphs, etc., and greatly detailed. Columns and heavy molding were characteristic of the period.
- **Chippendale, 1750 – 1790:** The wood of choice was mahogany. Maple, cherry, and walnut also continued to sell. Chippendale originated in England and took its name from the famous designer Thomas Chippendale. Intricately carved details are inspired by Chinese and French designs. Detailed ball and claw feet were found on the bottom of curved cabriole legs. Other legs may

be straight with a hairy paw on the end. The acanthus leaf may be repeated on examples of this period.

- Colonial, 1500-1800: Historically the Age of Exploration and Discovery started in the 1500s. The search for land or gold led colonists to seek new lives on new frontiers. Furniture built during this period of world history used native materials and was designed to meet the needs of the local population. It was simple and sturdy. Brass had to be imported so hardware was iron and made by local blacksmiths. In America the woods of choice were ash, maple, pine, walnut, and birch.
- Cottage: Cottage reflects more of a feeling of home and nature than a time period. Mass-produced during the mid-1800s, cottage was produced for functional use and not for aesthetic reasons. Furniture should have curved lines and may have used distressed wood. Glass knobs adorn its cabinets. Usually painted rather than stained, the legs were turned and a split back was common. Old barn wood and wicker can be added to create a cottage feeling.
- Eastlake, 1870-1890: Author Charles Eastlake wrote his book *Hints on Household Taste in Furniture, Upholstery, and Other Details*, published in 1868 as a backlash to the excesses of the Victorian style in fashion. His thoughts were that a simple design, characterized by straight lines and modest curves was far more elegant than Victorian excess. Pieces also displayed highly incised Middle and Far Eastern ornamentation, trestles, and brackets. American manufacturers found this minimal style easy to manufacture by machinery. Charles Eastlake tried to disassociate himself from the cheaply made American furniture that bears his name. Walnut, cherry, and oak were the preferred woods used.
- Empire (Classical, Napoleonic), 1805-1815: First introduced during the time of Napoleon, furniture of the period looked back at Egyptian, Greek, and Roman grandeur. Furniture made from rosewood, mahogany, and ebony was massive and trimmed in brass and bronze. The use of stenciling was popular. The style was resurrected in 1920 when archeologists opened

King Tut's tomb. American designers used American themes with patriotic symbols such as the eagle. Woods may have been painted black for dramatic effect. Feet were the extension of the flowing leg or ornamental such as the foot carved to resemble an animal claw or paw.
- Federal (Hepplewhite), 1780-1815: Influenced by British designer, Robert Adams, architecturally based on symmetry, the Federal style reflected the new feeling of patriotism in the former colonies. Mahogany and mahogany veneer continued to reign foremost, followed by native woods such as fruitwood, satinwood, and bird's eyes and ripple-grain maple. Pieces were augmented by inlays, paint, and shallow carving. Legs were straight or tapered forward. Feet were sometimes a continuation of the leg, rounded like a bulb, or a rectangular spade shape, which was larger at the top than at the bottom. Known masters of the time were Duncan Phyfe of New York, Samuel McIntire of Salem, and Seymour of Boston.
- French Restoration, 1830-1850: A subcategory of the Victorian, it was named after the period in which the Bourbon family attempted to regain the throne of France. Styles are plain and the introduction of bolster pillows and upholstery were introduced. French Restoration was only popular in the larger American cities such as New York and Boston.
- Gothic Revival, 1840-1860: Another subcategory of the Victorian Period, designs contained themes found in the 12th to 16th century European cultures. Walnut and oak furniture displayed turrets, quatrefoils, and arches and the re-emergence of carving.
- Mission Style: Simple designs made of rough sawn lumber and put together with pegs and dowels. Included in the Arts and Crafts period, pieces are functional and contain negligible ornamentation.
- Modern, 1925-1950: An extreme branch of the Art Deco movement, it was designed to be simple and functional. New materials were introduced such as plastic, molded plywood, and polished metal. Designers looked to the future rather than the past.

- Naturalistic, 1850-1914: Took on the look of the Rococo with more detail. One major accomplishment in the manufacture of furniture was the introduction of the wood lamination process. Upholstered pieces were often tufted.
- Queen Ann, 1720-1760: An American style that reached popularity in the late 1700's. Walnut was still the wood of choice with cherry and mahogany gaining popularity. The most relevant feature introduced is the cabriole leg (see next chapter).
- Rococo Revival, 1845-1870: Scrolls and "C" and "S" curves were the main design elements. Carved roses, scallop shells, flowers, and other naturalistic items added to the ornamentation. Legs and feet were cabriole or scrolling. Mahogany, rosewood, and walnut were favored woods. Less expensive varieties were often painted to appear a more expensive variety of wood.
- Shaker, 1790: Furniture produced by an austere communal religious society that came to the United States in 1774. Both practical and functional, the Shaker chair with its straight back is typical of the simple grace of early lines. The South Communal Family in New York opened a chair factory in 1860. Each chair was made by hand. After the Philadelphia Centennial Exposition of 1876, the Shakers increased their volume of production. Boring machines were introduced to make holes for rungs and slats. The Shaker colonies no longer exist, but the furniture design they created is still in production.
- Sheraton, 1790-1810: A cousin of the Federal, although created in a plainer simpler design. Based on the English designer, Thomas Sheraton, many pieces were constructed by rural cabinetmakers. Inlay was still popular. Legs were normally straight with the feet being an extension of the leg. Pine was added to previously mentioned woods.
- Victorian, 1805-1890: Ornate heavy utilitarian pieces made by hand. Carved ornamental aspects replaced by applied carving. Mass production was successfully introduced in America. Wavy molding and marble tops became popular. Black walnut and other local

hardwoods were used by country artisans. Mahogany and black walnut were found in more expensive pieces. Turned legs ended in carved bracket feet.
- William and Mary, 1689-1730: An American style made popular in the late 1600's. The main woods used were walnut and maple. Furniture veneering was introduced in this period. Club feet were prominent. Think of the shape of the head of a golf club driver.

The Rattan Chair

And that ye study to be quiet, and to do your own business, and to work with your own hands, as we commanded you; That ye may walk honestly toward them that are without, and that ye may have lack of nothing. 1 Thessalonians 11-12

It's funny what memories are forever etched on our human data discs. The only Christmases that remain clear in my mind were not ones where we got lots of presents; we never had lots of presents. No, the three I have retained clear memories of are centered around family. This is one of those.

When I was in elementary school, we left Massachusetts and were stationed at Travis Air Force Base in California. We had been there about two years when dad's Uncle Ralph came to live with us. He took my room. I was not a girlie girl so giving him my room was not a big deal. My folks closed in the patio and made that my room. Well, I did care when the wind blew our trellised rose bushes and the thorns scraped on the window panes making me think monsters were after me.

Uncle Ralph seemed really old and sad. He was my grandpa's older brother and would have been in his early seventies at the time. His wife and two sons had passed on decades before. Ralph's two brothers, and my dad, and his siblings were his only living relatives. Even an eight year-old understands how having no immediate family can be very lonely.

That Christmas was special. My sister and I got up at dawn and quietly crept to the living room. Screams ensued. Two child-size rattan chairs sat by the tree. One for each of us giggling girls. Each chair contained a Betsy McCall baby doll with a red ribbon around her neck. We each sat in our chair and hugged our new baby. No, it didn't bother us that we got the same thing. Mom was still dressing us like twins, although we were sixteen months apart. Uncle Ralph laughed and hugged us like we were his own granddaughters.

Mom later said Uncle Ralph really took a shine to me, but my tomboy exuberance wore him out. He stayed until the spring and then flew back to Pennsylvania. I know he left with fond memories of his stay. My grandpa told me so.

I loved sitting in my rattan chair. It reminded me of Christmas and Uncle Ralph.

Share memories of our elders with our children and grandchildren. Warm our hearts with their love and our enduring love for them. I pray I have created loving memories for my children and grandchildren to embrace when I have gone Home.

Trivia: In 2009 Greek shipping billionaire, Dinos Martinos, purchased a chair by Irish designer Eileen Gray. She created it sometime between 1917 and 1919. Martinos bought the "Dragon Chair" for $27.8 million dollars, making it the most expensive chair in the world.

Terminology:

- Acanthus: A plant of the Mediterranean region, its leaf if often depicted in the scroll motifs or borders in art and architecture. It is a symbol of enduring life. It was often found in the Classical, Federal, Georgian Revival, and Empire periods.
- Apron/skirt: A plain or ornamented strip used to connect the legs on tables and chairs.
- Ball foot: A round foot that resembled a bun.
- Bail handle: The handle of a drawer pull. Introduced in the William and Mary period it is normally brass or glass and hangs down from a reversed half moon brass mount.
- Banderol: A decorative element that resembled a long scroll or ribbon. It often contained an inscription or emblem.
- Banding: Popular during the 1700s, banding was a decorative border or edging of contrasting veneer.
- Bow front: A chest with a slight outward swell (bow) in the middle of the front.
- Bracket: A configuration placed on the bottom of a vertical surface to provide either structural or visual support.

- Breakfront: A piece where the center section protrudes beyond the other adjoining sections.
- Buffet (sideboard, server): A piece of dining room furniture used to store linens and silverware.
- Burl: A large outgrowth, normally round in shape, growing on the trunk or limb of a tree. Wood from the outgrowth is used as decorative veneer.
- Cabinet: A French word for closet or cupboard like repository.
- Cabriole leg: Designed after the S-shape of an animal's leg, it is able to support heavy pieces on its slim legs without stretchers. It concluded in an ornamental foot. They were very popular in the first half of the 18th century.
- Candlestand (tea) tables: Small pedestal based tables used to hold candles, knick knacks, or other small items in a room.
- Cane chair: The seat and/or back of the chair is plaited with stems of cane, palms, or plants such as bamboo. They were popular in America in the late 1600s.
- Chest-on-chests (highboys): Introduced in the Chippendale era, these pieces are one chest setting on a second chest. They may be almost 7' tall and require a stool to reach the top drawers.
- Cinquefoil: A five-lobed circle or arch found in Gothic designs.
- Claw-and-ball foot: The foot of a piece of furniture carved in the shape of a bird's claw clutching a ball.
- Club foot: Curved head that resembles the head of a driver (wood) in a set of golf clubs.
- Commode: This important piece of furniture served as a dry sink, washstand, and repository for a chamber pot before indoor plumbing.
- Cupboard: A piece designed for storage before built-in closets appeared. Usually there were two pieces. The top piece displayed treasured items and the bottom stored china or silverware. It was designed in a wedge shape to fit a corner or straight to set against a wall.
- Cusps: The point where foils meet in Gothic designs.

- Dovetail: Wedge shaped grooves designed to interlock to produce a secure joint when joining front and sides of drawers.
- Ebonizing: Using a lesser quality of wood and staining it to appear as ebony.
- Ebony: A deep black hard wood native to Africa, Mauritius, and Ceylon. It was one of the first woods to be used as a veneer.
- Étagère: An elegant standing or hanging shelf unit for displaying knick knacks, etc.
- Feet: Found at the end of the leg, it provides balance to the object.
- Finial: A design element (ornamental structure), either carved or turned, placed at a termination point.
- Foil: French for "leaf." In Gothic design it is the leaf-shaped curve between cusps inside an arch or circle.
- Fluting: A shallow vertical groove found on a column.
- Game table: A small table meant to play chess or cards.
- Gate leg table: A drop-leaf table with rounded or oval end that can be folded down and opened to save space. A leg swings out to hold the folded drop-leaf area when opened.
- Gesso: Whiting and glue mixed in water.
- Gilded: A layer of thin pure gold leaf was applied. Usually used on mirrors.
- Graining: Applying paint to make the grain appear something other than its origin.
- Handholds: The arm support of a chair where you can rest your arms and hands.
- Hoosier cabinet: A type of kitchen unit popular in the 1900s. It contained a large work area surrounded by bins that held flour, sugar, etc. It took its name from the Hoosier Manufacturing Company of New Castle, Indiana where most of the cabinets were made.

- Inlay (Marquetry): A decorative process where the design is cut into the piece and then filled in with another material to create the resulting pattern. The secondary material may be veneer, metal, mother-of-pearl, etc.
- Knee: The upper curve of a cabriole leg.
- Knuckle: The end of the arm of a chair that resembles a human knuckle.
- Lacquer: A varnish which contains the sap of the Rhus tree. A popular finish used in Oriental designs.
- Ladder-back (slat-back) chair: The back of the chair resembles the rungs of a ladder. Popular in the 17th and 18th century rural home.
- Laminated: Layers of wood glued together to form a plank of wood. Normally an expensive wood is layered onto a lesser expensive wood.
- Lozenge: A diamond shaped pattern.
- Lyre: A motif based on the stringed instrument of Greece: A particular favorite of designer Duncan Phyfe.
- Mahogany: A hardwood found in South America, Central America, and Africa. The Caribbean variety is considered the highest quality. During the 18th century, mahogany replaced walnut as the preferred wood for furniture and was extensively used for veneer.
- Maple: A pale hardwood found plentiful in northern America, it became the wood of colonial America. Bird's eye maple is the most sought after. Older maple has a rich warm honey color. Maple eventually became a secondary choice and was used for under framing and less expensive furniture.
- Marlborough leg: A straight or fluted leg that ends with a block foot. A favorite of Chippendale.
- Marquetry: The process of applying different woods to create a design pattern.
- Medallion: A circular, oval, or square design element molded, struck, stamped or cast with an insignia or other artistic motif to be applied to, inlaid, or painted on another object.

- Monopodium: Often found protruding from a cornucopia, it was a foot of a leg of furniture carved to resemble an animal foot. Found during the Empire period.
- Muntin: Strips of wood that hold panes of glass in a glazed door. Ex. Glass front secretaries or china cabinets. They may be merely functional or decorative.
- Ormolu: The word "or" is French for "gold." Molu translates to "mashed." Ormolu was gilded architectural details that were made of bronze or brass and then gilded. For furniture these details were moldings and medallions.
- Pad foot: Similar to a club foot. Shaped like the head of a golf driver with a disk underneath.
- Palmette: A motif reflecting the fan-shaped leaves of a palm tree.

- Parquetry: Pieces of veneer are used to create patterns.
- Patera: An oval or round ornamentation such as a rosette, carved, inlaid, painted, or incised on a piece.
- Patina: The change in a surface that occurs because of wear, age, and care. In wood the change is beneficial in determining the value of a piece.
- Pearling: A design created by a series of rounded forms, either the same size or graduated sizes. Normally found in brass mounts.
- Pie safe: A type of cupboard with tin hand-pierced door panels.
- Piecrust molding: Fluted molding that resembles the edges of a piecrust.

- Pull brackets: Arms placed on each side of a surface pulled out for use, such as the writing surface of a secretary. Once pulled out the brackets provide support.
- Quarter sawn oak: At the mill the oak log is cut in half. Then the half is sawn in half to form the four quarters. Finally, the wood is cut on the diagonal from the middle of the piece towards the edge. This method of preparing the wood reveals the stripe or "ray" of oak and renders the wood stronger. It was popular in the Arts & Crafts and Prairie periods.
- Rail: The horizontal section of a chair frame that is at the top of the chair, across the middle, and on the seat section. It provides support as well as design.

- Rattan: A type of wicker native to Indonesia.
- Reed(ing): The opposite of fluting, reeding is a design element that resembles rope molding. It was used extensively on furniture legs and feet.
- Rush: A type of cattail reed preferred by chair seat weavers.
- Saber leg: A type of chair leg shaped to resemble a cavalry saber.
- Secretary: The 17th and 18th century version of a desk with storage units.
- Serpentine: The center of the piece resembles an "S' snakelike figure and flanked by concave ends.
- Shoe: The part of the back seat rail of a chair that maintains support or the bottom of the splat.
- Slat: The horizontal piece of wood used in chairs to provide support. Example: The back of a ladder chair is constructed of several slats.
- Splat: The center wooden back rest section of a chair is called a splat.

- Stretcher: A wooden crosspiece on tables and chairs to connect the legs for added support.
- Tambour: A flexible roll cover such as on a rolltop desk or a sliding door on a cabinet.
- Tilt-top table: The top surface of the table was hinged so that the table took very little space when not in use.
- Turning: An element of the piece formed by the rotation of a wooden dowel on a lathe. The lathe shaped the dowel into the desired design.
- Veneer: Slices of wood ranging from 1/16" and 1/32" of a quality wood applied over a lesser decorative wood.
- Wassily chair: The first chair using tubular steel.
- Wicker: Strips of wood woven into indoor and outdoor furniture, screens, and baskets. Popular in the Victorian era, wicker was inspired by Oriental imports.
- Windsor chair: A spindled backed wooden chair with a sculpted seat. Its back reclines slightly.

A Penny for Your Thoughts

Then shalt thou call, and the Lord shall answer; thou shalt cry, and He shall say, Here I am.   Isaiah 58:9

When my mom gave me her Grandma Phipps's family Bible, I was ecstatic. All the sections recording the births, marriages, and deaths of family members were intact aiding in completing information for my genealogy research.

Tucked away between pages were some wonderful surprises. Great-grandma Phipps's and Great-aunt Margaret had saved postcards they received or sent others during their lives in rural Oklahoma. These jewels give first-hand inklings into the personality of the people who penned them.

My favorite was a World War I postcard my Great-uncle Leo mailed to his future wife, my beloved Great-aunt Margaret, letting her know his outfit was moving. He signed it, "I love you." This display of emotion was unusual for the time. It makes me smile to know he loved her enough to express it on a postcard. That meant half the county knew he loved her before the sentiment was delivered to his sweetheart's door.

At the end of the nineteenth and into the early twentieth century party-line phones and postcards were the two major forms of communication. It's hard to imagine in this era of cell phones and text messaging that anyone would want to use a postcard. Plenty are collecting them.

Deltiology, postcard collecting, is one of the largest collectable hobbies in the world. Stamp and coin collecting are the other two. Postcards chronicle our history. They are available at reasonable prices and divided into numerous categories. The world's first adhesive postage stamp, called the Penny Black, was issued in England in 1840. The one cent stamp was black with a white portrait of Queen Victoria. American collectors are primarily interested in American produced postcards so that is our subject.

Praise you for providing me access to a tender moment from my aunt and uncle's courtship. Love is the foundation of a happy home and caring family. It comforts me to know they were truly blessed.

> **Trivia**: "Hand Tinted" postcards were of various topics, printed in black and white, and colored by hand. As they became more popular "assembly-line-style" production was established in France and Belgium. Each woman was given one color to add to the postcard as it passed. Women would wet their brush in their mouths to form a tip. Soon the lead based paint made factory workers ill ending the manufacturing process.

Postcards are cataloged in these categories:

- Pre-postcard Era (1840-1869). The ancestor of what we know as a private postal card was copyrighted by John P. Chariton of Philadelphia in 1861. His copyright was transferred to H. L. Lipman and labeled "Lipman's Postal Card, Patent Applied For." They were marketed until 1873.
- Pioneer Era (1870-1898) cards were produced before July 1, 1898. Designs were printed onto Government Postal cards or private card stock. Early postcards didn't have the line going down the back of the card to separate the address from the message. By law you could not write on the address side of these cards. This forced the sender to write a message across the artwork on the front. These are referred to as "undivided" cards. The first card printed as a souvenir in the United States was created in 1893 for the World's Columbian Exposition in Chicago.
- Early Century (1898 – About 1918) cards are regarded as the "Golden Age" of postcard publishing. On May 19, 1898, Congress passed the Private Mailing Card Act

which allowed private publishers to produce postcards. Although their cards were to be called "souvenir cards" and labeled "Private Mailing Cards" a new industry was created. European printing houses produced the majority of stock. The two most desired are Raphael Tuck (England) and Paul Finkenrath of Berlin (PFB-German). Many successful American printers had their paper stock produced in Europe and are imprinted "Made in Bavaria." In 1906 Eastman Kodak sold an affordable camera called the "Folding Pocket Camera." This invention allowed the public to print their own photographs right onto postcard backs introducing the Real Photo Era. On March 1, 1907, the U.S. Post Office allowed the public to write on the address side of a postcard initiating the "divided back" card. The American public embraced the picture postcard. The U.S. Post Office reported 677 million postcards were mailed for their fiscal year ending June 1908. That was thirty-two postcards for every man, woman, and child living in the United States in 1908.

- Mid Century also called the Early Modern Period (1915-1930) was ushered in when World War I stopped the importation of German stock. After the war ended, the destruction of factories and original art ended German dominance of the market. Business dwindled except for the "Real Photo" version. Americans were becoming "kings of the road." Racks of beautiful picture postcards were available to send home to chronicle their journey.
- Linen Era (1930-1944) provided an improved picture printed on a linen type paper stock. World War II created a shortage of materials. The high cost of the manufacturing in the U.S. prompted the "white borders" on the card to save ink.
- Chrome Era (1950 – Present) "Photochrome" or "Chrome" postcards were launched by the Union Oil Company. They contained images of Western states and were given away in the oil company's Union 76 service stations with purchases.

There are other factors that determine the value of a postcard other than age. Here are additional points that affect price:

Condition: Excellent mint condition demands the highest price. Creases, tears, round corners, or smudges may make an otherwise high value card worth only half the price.

Topic: Rare cards are harder to find and exact a higher price. A Thanksgiving card would be rarer than an Easter or Christmas postcard. A color card would draw more interest than a black and white. Was the card published en mass or a small local shop for local consumption?

If you check the Internet you will find hundreds of sites for collectors both national and international. One I found very informative is:

www.metropostcard.com

Mi Familia, My Family

Children's children are the crown of old men; and the glory of children are their fathers.   Proverbs 17:6

My favorite family photograph was taken in front of my grandparents' fieldstone house in Pennsylvania when I was two years old. I love it because it shows my paternal great-grandparents, grandparents, my dad's siblings, their spouses and children. It gives me a sense of kinship to those individuals I did not have a chance to spend much time with over the years. My great-grandparents were in their eighties when I was born. I have only one clear memory of them.

Pittsburgh can be very cold and snowy at Christmas. Mom and Grandma were busy in the kitchen putting away the few leftovers from our traditional Christmas feast. There was no television in the house so the men were sitting around drinking coffee and discussing the Pittsburgh Steelers' record for the year. Great-grandma Thorn leaned over and whispered in Aunt Mary Eileen's ear. Mary Eileen got up and moved to the piano. Soon music filled the room. Talented, and not-so-talented, family members took turns performing. The laughter and affection of that day wrapped me in a warm loving memory I still feel today.

During this visit Great-granddad Thorn took my mother aside. He handed her a small box with a monogrammed gold brooch. The initials on the pin were "ELT." "This was my mother's," he said as he handed her the small box. "My mother's name was Emma Llewellyn Thorn. You and she have the same initials. I want you to have this."

Fifteen years ago when I started doing the family genealogy, my mom passed this brooch on to me. This spring I passed it on to a beloved niece, Erin Thorn. It felt right that another "ET" should wear our great-great-grandmother's brooch.

Gold jewelry has long been a favorite of men and women alike. Gold necklaces have been found dating back to 7th century BC. During this time of financial insecurity more and more people are parting with their family treasures. It is unfortunate that many items of the past will be lost. However, new treasures will be defined and passed on to our grandchildren. What little girl wouldn't love having grandma's 1960s gold tone mood ring with the adjustable band? Little Kyle will be surprised when he opens the box of classic cufflinks made from buffalo nickels mounted on chrome plated hinged backs. 'What are cufflinks used for?" He questions innocently. What he really wanted was the plastic model of the Starship Enterprise hanging in grandpa's study. "Beam me up, Scottie."

Families give us the sense of who we are. They guide us and help us find the true meaning of our lives here on Earth. Their gifts cannot be measured in dollars and cents, but the richness they bring to our daily lives.

Today, Italy is the leader in gold jewelry manufacturing and the United States is the largest market.

Karat – The word "karat" (abbreviated Kt) indicates the proportion of solid gold in an alloy based on a total of 24 parts. Example: 14-karat (14K) gold signifies a configuration of 14 parts of gold and 10 parts of other metals. Pure gold is a very soft metal, a 2.5 – 3 on the industry standard, the Mohs Scale, and is mixed with other elements to be sturdy and easier to craft. Carat with a "C" denotes gem weight.

- 24K: Considered pure gold, no alloys added. Very expensive and soft.
- 22K: 91.6% Popular in Asia. Still very soft.
- 20K: 83.3% Noted for its bright color.
- 18K: 75% Most popular in European countries.
- 14K: 58.3% Most popular gold sold in United States.
- 12K: 50% Seldom seen since 1932 when 14K standard established.
- 10K: 41.7% The minimum karat in U.S that can still be called gold.

- 9K: 37.5% Popular in Ireland and minimum karat gold in Canada.
- 8K: 33.3% The minimum gold karat in Mexico.

Alloys used to strengthen gold may also change its color:
- Yellow Gold—Copper and Silver.
- White Gold—Nickel, Zinc, Silver, Platinum, and Palladium.
- Pink (Rose) Gold—Copper.
- Green Gold—Silver, Copper, and Zinc.
- Blue Gold—Iron.

Terminology:
- Aqua Regia: A 3:1 mixture of hydrochloric acid and nitric acid used to test platinum and gold.
- Ductile: A substance easily pulled or stretched into a thin wire. Gold is the most ductile metal.
- Electroplated: Plating solution must have at least seven millionths of an inch of gold. Electroplating (also called Galvanotechnics after its inventor, Luigi Galvani) is a process by which metals are bonded using electricity. Electrogilded coating is the thinnest (less than 0.000007 inches thick). Gold-plated metals have a coating thicker than 0.000007 inches.
- Fineness: A means of denoting the purity of gold and silver alloys. It is expressed in parts per thousand. Example: An alloy containing 75% gold is expressed as "750". The United States and Great Britain use "K", karat, a fraction of 24, which is pure gold. 18 K would be 18/24 ="750" or 75%.
- Gold filled jewelry: Made from a base metal, usually brass, that has a thin sheet of gold laminated to the surface. For example, jewelry marked 1/20 G.F. 12 Kt. is at least 1/20th gold and is layered with 12 karat gold. To be classified as gold-filled, a piece must be at least 1/20 gold by weight. Pieces are marked G.F. or "doublé d'or".
- Gold leaf: Gold produced in a thin layer to be placed on an item to make it appear gold.

- Gold plated: Items that have a very thin layer of gold usually applied by electroplating. Pieces are marked G.E.P., gold electroplate, gold plated, or electro-plaqué d'or.
- Gold washed also called flash gold: The plating solution (0.2 micron) falls short of the electroplating gold standard.
- Hallmark: An official mark (or a series of marks) made to signify the fineness of the metal and the manufacturer's mark. Other hallmarks indicate the maker of the piece, ex. Paul Revere, and sometimes the year of manufacture, ex. 1775.
- Rolled gold: Like gold filled a very thin sheet of gold is laminated to a lesser metal (usually brass). The two layers of metal are heated under pressure to bond them. The combined metals are then rolled into a very thin sheet and crafted into jewelry or other items. Rolled gold pieces are marked rolled gold plate, R.G.P., or plaqué d'or laminé.
- Troy weight: Gold, platinum, and silver are measured in troy weight. Troy weight also has units of pennyweights, ounces, and pounds; however, they are not the equivalent of our normal units of measure.

  Troy Weight—Equivalence
  1 pennyweight—24 grains = 1.5552 grams
  1 Troy ounce = 20 pennyweight—31.1035 grams
  1 Troy pound = 12 Troy ounces—373.24 grams
- Vermeil: Gold-plated silver. Vermeil is seldom produced due to the price of silver.

There are many things to consider before having Grandma's necklace melted for the gold. Make sure you are working with a reputable firm and that you understand the terminology used. Don't google today's gold price and think that's what you will get. We are normally working with grams not ounces. Don't be disappointed. Do the homework.

Trivia: Ancient Egyptians were some of the first to fashion a solid gold band to represent marriage. Their culture believed the circle symbolized the eternity of marriage. It's estimated that world wide more than 19 tons of gold are fashioned into wedding rings each year.

Look for the Silver Lining

And the Lord spake unto Moses saying, "Make thee two trumpets of silver; of a whole piece shalt thou make them; that thou mayest use them for the calling of the assembling, and for the journeying of the camp."

Numbers 10:1-2

Several years ago Mom and I headed out to our favorite flea market, Perkiomenville Auction and Flea Market, in Perkiomenville, Pennsylvania. We parked her van and started setting up for early customers. Now, when I say early I mean it was 5:00 a.m. and still pitch black outside.

I unloaded the back of the van as other dealers checked out what Mom brought today. Some dickered on the price. Mom always enjoyed this part of the process the most. She teased them and told them they were trying to take advantage of her, then the real bargaining started. Mom stopped long enough to help me lift the oak dresser and set it in the most advantageous spot. Next was a Victorian mahogany china cabinet. Last were assorted boxes of linens, art pottery, primitive stoneware, in other words, just about anything that could possibly sell.

Yes, I fully understood I was her manual labor. That was okay. I knew in two hours I would take off and walk the acre of booths and shop to my heart's content. I wanted a nice set of silverware to use when company came. This was the right place to find it at a reasonable price.

Flea marketing was and is genetic. I really loved visiting each table, picking up an item and examining it, then bartering for a good price. After a couple of hours, I returned to a table I had visited earlier and bought a twelve-place setting of monogrammed silverware in a tarnish free case for $50. Wahoo, I was excited.

About 2:00 p.m. we loaded what didn't sell and started home. Mom and I unloaded the van and then headed for a couch in the living room. Stretched out we traded stories about what we'd done that day. I told her about my great find and she asked to see them. "That's a good buy," she said as she closed the case. "You know I always planned on giving you Aunt Margaret's Rogers silverware." No, I didn't know. Mom got up and went into the dining room. When she returned she had a silver chest of William Roger's Anniversary silver. More importantly, it had been my Great-aunt Margaret's.

I went home from Pennsylvania that year with two sets of silver. One I bought and the other passed down from someone I loved. Nothing is better than touching an item that brings back wonderful memories. I still love and miss my, Aunt Margaret.

It is comforting to know that the people we love who have left this world will be there in the next. I strive each day to live a proper life so I may see them again. I know I have been forgiven for my many sins.

Next to gold, silver has been the second favorite precious metal used to make jewelry and other valued objects. Archaeological digs have found ancient coins and even a suit of silver plated armor.

Hippocrates (known as the Father of Medicine) used silver to heal wounds. During the Middle Ages royalty used silver tableware, drank from silver cups, and developed a slight blue skin tone. Hence they were referred to as "blue bloods." The peasant population noticed that fewer blue bloods were dying of the plague and assumed silver protected them making silver household items even more desirable.

Modern scientists determined that low levels of silver in water kill some strains of bacteria. The antimicrobial properties of silver come from its ionized form, Ag+. The Ag+ in silver keep bacteria and parasites from assimilating oxygen; the result is bacteria suffocate and die. The bluish skin tone referred to as argyria is considered a symptom of an adverse heavy metal poisoning.

Cultured Victorian homes in both England and America reflected the new emerging middle class and their demand for the finer things once affordable only to the aristocracy. Silverware, always a sign of breeding, was ornate and essential to set a proper table. Each course had specialized implements, including such items as an asparagus server, a berry spoon, or fish knives and forks.

American Victorian (1860-1890) silver plate is both available and affordable. Sterling collectors seek Gorham, and Reed & Barton as the benchmark of sterling silver manufacturing. Today's collector may set a table with several various designs of silver place settings. Unlike our Victorian grandmothers, we like the variety.

Several things to think about before buying:

Is the piece dented or damaged? Do the dents need repair. Repairing the piece can be more expensive than the price you paid.

Is it a true item of the period? Know your hallmarks.

Is it sterling or silver plated? Check the hallmark. Silver will say silver. Silver plated items may or may not show a hallmark.

In 2010 Mexico passed Peru as the world's largest silver producing nation. China followed with Australia and Chile in close pursuit. Continued demand for silver can only increase as new ways are discovered to use its full potential in medicine and industry.

Terminology:

- Amalgam: A combination of mercury and silver, gold, copper or another metal used for centuries. A major use is in dentistry.
- Britannia: The recognized standard used in the UK of silver defined by law as 95.8% pure silver in a 1000. First introduced in the UK in 1697, its purpose was to discontinue the widespread melting down of sterling silver coinage. The figure of Britannia replaced traditional sterling hallmark of a lion passant. The sterling standard returned to law in 1720. This is softer than sterling and may have a faint blue color.
- Bruise: A dent.
- Cleaning: Best washed in soap and water and dried with a soft cloth. Don't put in the dishwasher and don't leave wet. Use non abrasive cleansers to remove tarnish.
- Commercial Silver: Normally shipped in 1000 oz. bars and is 99.9% or higher.

- Doré Bullion: An impure alloy of silver and gold produced at a mine. Ex. 65% gold and 35% silver
- Doré Silver: Crude silver that still contains an amount of gold.
- Electroplating: A method of adhering a layer of pure silver on a base metal by electrolysis.
- Embossing: A decoration achieved by pushing metal from underneath a layer to create a raised pattern.
- Engraving: Removing metal by scraping or cutting away to create a design.
- Filigree: Delicate silver and gold wirework used as decorative panels.
- Flatware: Term for tableware constructed from a single, flat piece of silver.
- Frosted silver: Technique using sulphuric acid to create a white matte finish silver. Used as a contrasting decorative layer on the surface of sterling silver.
- Grain: One grain is 64.799 milligrams. An early unit of weight based on the weight of one grain of wheat taken from the middle of the ear of wheat.
- Hallmarking: An early consumer protection process, the stamped letter or emblem shows the piece was tested at an assay office and it meets the standard of purity, 92.5% silver.
- Hallmarks: A group of distinctive marks applied to an item of silver to describe standard, manufacturer, may also reflect date crafted, and country of origin. English silver may contain the imprint of a king or queen's head to indicate that the taxes were paid.
- Hollowware: Items made from silver that you can put things in such as bowls, creamers, vases, and often the handles of knives were hollowware.
- Leopard's Head: 1300 to 1856 the London mark used on sterling silver.
- Lion Passant: The standing or a rearing lion used as a hallmark that signifies the piece is sterling and English.

- Pacific cloth: A cloth you can purchase that prevents tarnish and is used for storing silver.
- Paul de Lamerie: (1688-1751) 18th century London silversmith of Huguenot origin. His works are highly sought after by collectors.
- Plate: Traditional term for articles manufactured in silver and gold. Sheffield Plate in the early 18th century resulted in a term, meaning the plating being on any base metal.
- Sheffield Plate: Plating copper with sterling silver developed by Thomas Boulsover of Sheffield, England in 1740. Close examination reveals the copper underneath. Items can range in value from hundreds to thousands of dollars.
- Silver-gilt: An application of a thin layer of silver for decorative purposes or as protection against corrosion.
- Sterling standard: 92.5% pure silver is the recognized standard in the UK and America. (925 parts pure silver in a 1000) Standards vary throughout the world. Some countries have higher standards, others lower such as 800 parts per 1000.
- Troy Ounce or weight: French system of weight. One troy ounce equals 31.1034 grammes.
- Vermeil: French term for silver gilt and used in fashionable costume jewelry in the 1940s, 50s and 60s.

Trivia: A 13-year-old French Huguenot immigrated to the New World to seek an apprenticeship as a silversmith. Apollos Rivoire anglicized the family name to became Paul Revere, Sr. (1702-1754). His son inherited his shop and went on to become a well-known patriot and Boston's most famous and successful silversmith. Paul Revere fathered sixteen children, by two wives. His sons joined him in trade and his business grew and diversified. His repertoire ran from bell and cannon founder, dentistry, and owner of the first copper rolling mill in North America (1801). His company provided copper sheeting for the hull of the U.S.S. Constitution. Although owned by Corning, Revere Copper and Brass, Inc. remains in business today and produces "Revere Ware" the copper bottomed cookware.

Three Generations of Noritake

I will give you the good of the land of Egypt, and you shall eat the fat of the land.   Genesis 45:18

When my paternal grandmother passed away in 1973, there in the corner of her basement her heirs found four complete sets of china. Each twelve piece setting was still in the original packing boxes. One set was stamped "Noritake." My mom spied them right away. We brought them back from Japan in 1950. My dad served in the Air Force as part of the post war Army of Occupation of Japan. Noritake china was the nicest thing a serviceman could bring home to his mama. My mom also brought a set home for our family. You can still open my mom's cupboard and find a piece or two left of the white Wedding Band designed porcelain. It must be a family tradition. I brought mine, the Reina pattern, back to the U.S. from Okinawa in 1969.

Upon their discovery, my uncles and aunts speculated that when the wonderful gifts were given to her, she didn't want to disappoint her son or daughter by saying she already had a set. Grandma accepted them graciously and stored them for decades in the dark basement to be retrieved at a later date by the giver. She was like that.

In my eyes, my Grandma Thorn will always serve as the epitome of the perfect grandmother. When we came running through the kitchen door, the aroma of fresh baked homemade potato bread filled our senses. Each grandchild stood patiently as Grandma sliced the soft warm loaf she had removed from the oven. We lined up to get a generous serving of real butter, not that new oleo margarine stuff, but real butter that melted into your luscious piece of baked heaven. That was how contemporary women expressed love – through baked goods.

As a young woman she graduated from college with a degree in teaching, quite an accomplishment for a woman in 1920. She knew God had a plan for her life. He did. She was a leader is her church, a leader in Eastern Star, and still taught Sunday school when she died. Each woman in her Sunday school class received an African violet from the plant stand in her kitchen.

I cannot speak about my grandma without mentioning her hugs. Strong warm arms encircled you and pressed your little child body into her chest. There is no doubt that those arms will be open and ready for me when I enter Heaven. I can't wait to be wrapped in that love again.

My church provides me with people in my life who model the principles of a true Christian woman. May I follow their example. May I display their grace. Help me become the woman I know I can be.

Noritake China: Chinaware first manufactured in 1904 in Nagoya, Japan, by the Nippon Toki Kaisha Company for the Morimura Brothers Trading Company. This high-quality line of ceramic products was produced for export to the United States. During WWII the factory was damaged and the poorer quality of product used the name "China Rose" from 1946-1948. During the post-war reconstruction decade, the factory reopened again and resumed the Noritake brand name. There are many patterns. Pieces should be marked "Noritake" with a wreath, "M," "N," and early pieces say "Nippon." Check the internet location www.noritakechina.com and click on Noritake Collectors Guild to see a guide to marks and samples of their art.

> **Hint**: I have packed and moved the set of Noritake I bought in Okinawa in 1969 at least six times. Pack anything you want in boxes from the grocery store etc., but spend the extra money and buy dish packs to pack your good dishes. Enfold each piece in white wrapping paper, newspapers leave a black residue, and then cover them again in bubble wrap. Buy the inserts to keep the contents from banging against each other and chipping the edges. Follow mover's suggestions regarding standing plates and bowls on their side and not flat in the box. This takes the weight and pressure off the center of the dish.

Give Me a Hug

And God made the beast of the earth after his kind, and cattle after their kind, and every thing that creepeth upon the earth after his kind: and God saw that it was good.

Genesis 1: 25

There is another Christmas I would like to share from my childhood. We never made lists or asked for anything. Whatever we got we appreciated. Each year we made popcorn, strung it, and draped it on the tree. Construction paper trees, ornaments, and stars dotted the green limbs. The scent of the cedar tree filled the room.

My sister and I went to bed early on Christmas Eve full of excitement. We woke the next morning and our feet hit the floor running. We saw them as soon as we entered the front room. Two giant teddy bears gazed back at us from under the tree. Mine was a dark brown with a big red bow around his neck. His black glass eyes looked right at me. How wonderful! That's all we got that Christmas, except for the socks and underwear in our stockings. We were thrilled. Each of us had our own teddy bear to hold close and love. I know I could feel his arms cuddle me back. A child loves like that.

Recollections of these early experiences enrich our later life; the Christmas present, the swimming medal, the spelling bee all made us the person now blessed. They remind us that the abundance in our lives are emotional and not economical. Christmas is a time of love, not a time to worry about buying expensive gifts The gift was Jesus.

For Americans the stuffed toy bear cub was named after our beloved President Theodore Roosevelt. In 1902 President Roosevelt went bear hunting with some friends in Mississippi and came back empty-handed. Some of his hunting companions caught a bear cub and tied it to a tree for him to shoot. He declined answering, "Spare the bear." Clifford Berryman, a political cartoonist chronicled the event in the *Washington Post*. A Brooklyn toymaker Morris Michtom, and his wife, Rose, produced a sweet bear cub they named "Teddy's Bear" and displayed it in their shop window with a copy of the cartoon. The Michtoms joined with the Ideal Novelty and Toy Company and a new craze was launched.

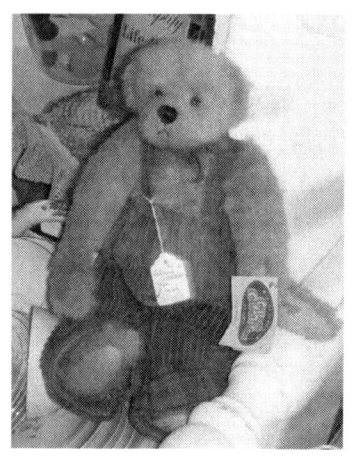

At the same time a disabled German seamstress named Margarete Steiff added a new plush bear to her toy menagerie based on a drawing by her nephew, a former art student. Richard's drawing more resembled a real bear with a long snout, hump back, long arms, and curved paws. His prototype resembled what he observed at the Stuttgart Zoo. In March of 1903, they introduced their first bear – Baer 55PB- at the Leipzig Toy Fair. Mohair in yellow, red, black, blue, green, and several shades of brown was used to create the bear's body. Glass or metal eyes were standard. Wood shavings, called excelsior, filled the toys to give them a soft feel, and allowed jointed movable arms and legs. Kapok replaced excelsior after World War I. Felt pads were hand sewn onto the paws and legs. Four claws are hand embroidered on the hands and feet. Each Steiff bear had a trademark button in the left ear to distinguish it from fakes. Known for its high quality, Steiff sold thousands of bears in the United States between 1903 and World War I. In 1907 alone, they manufactured 974,000 bears for a growing market.

New companies opened and closed during the period of 1910 to 1940 both in Europe and the United States. Many musical and mechanical toys were introduced. The outbreak of World War II ended production as the factories changed to support the war effort.

After the war the public wanted washable toys made from synthetic fibers. Plastic eyes replaced glass and foam rubber replaced kapok. The bear market was flooded with cheaper mass-produced teddy bears from the Far East. Beanie Babies of the 1990's introduced a new generation to the obsession of acquiring teddy bears.

Vintage collectors desire the handmade teddy bear made in the first decades of the twentieth century. In 1999 they bought $441 million worth of teddy bears to add to their hugs. Appropriately, hug is the name for a teddy bear collection. In 1994 *Teddy Girl* by Steiff sold at Christie's in London for $176,000. April 24, 2001, a one-of-a-kind Steiff bear sold for $193,477 to be displayed at a new museum in Jeju, Korea. There is an elusive green Steiff worth more than either of these two out there somewhere. Good hunting.

Trivia: Winnie the Pooh was a J. K. Farnell & Co. bear that Christopher Robin Milne received for his first birthday in 1921. Five years later his father, writer, A. A. Milne, published his first Winnie-the-Pooh book based on Christopher and his stuffed animals. The original toys are on display in the Central Children's Room of the Donnell Branch of the New York Public Library in New York City.

Occupied Japan

And they shall build the old wastes, they shall raise up the former desolations, and they shall repair the waste cities, the desolations of many generations.   Isaiah 61:4

A little out of focus and color that is lackluster never bothers me as I watch the film for the hundredth time. Here comes the frames chronicling Tokyo. A small car pulls over to the side of the road. The driver jumps out and runs to the back of the vehicle. He flips open the small door on a silo like apparatus strapped to the back bumper. Wood chips fall out into the small basket he grabbed from where it had been wedged. His right hand removes the top of a second silo. Steam escapes. He pours the basket of wood chips into the steam and drops to the ground to sweep up every chip on the road. Is this steam powered car Japan's newest experiment to end dependence on fossil fuels and put a stop to global warming?

No, this is a home movie taken by my father as he served in the Army of Occupation following the end of World War II. Our home was Tachikawa Air Force Base just outside of Tokyo. The Japanese people embraced us strange looking foreigners. My sister and I were fair with long blonde hair. The mamasans loved to feel the soft flaxen strands. My mom recalls one time at the Tokyo train station when there were so many Japanese flocked around us, she feared we would become separated.

At the end of the war the Japanese economy was devastated. General Douglas MacArthur was sent to Japan to help the people establish a new form of government and provide direction on how to retool their industries from military to commercial uses. During this period from 1945 to 1948, a new constitution was written stripping the Emperor of any military powers, and amongst other sections on racial equality and personal freedoms was one giving women the right to vote. Sweeping land reforms changed the agricultural face of Japan from tenant farmers toiling for rich lords to individual land owners.

Japanese pottery companies returned to manufacturing designs to export to Western countries to obtain hard currency. This period from 1945 until 1952 is referred to as "Occupied Japan." Resentment of the island nation remained high following the war. Retailers felt by adding the word "occupied" to the new stock, the buyer would feel they were contributing to a conquered nation rather than a warring one, making their purchase more palatable. Four versions of marks designate the item came from this period: "Japan", "Made in Japan", "Occupied Japan", and "Made in Occupied Japan". Only the last two marks guarantee the pieces were made in the true Occupied Japan period. For serious collectors, only these two marks will do. Two good resources for additional information are www.mcantiques.com and www.occupiedjapan.net. Here you can view manufacturers, their trademarks, and some samples of their wares.

The variety of items produced was diverse. Porcelain figurines are the most popular items for collectors, followed by cups and saucers, dishes, and ash trays. Vast quantities of Occupied Japan were produced, making it easy to find and reasonably priced.

As viewed in our home movies, my mom loved walking through the open air markets and buying the beautiful figurines and china. A pair of blue floral porcelain hibachis, Japanese for fire bowl, sat outside our front door as planters. The locals used them for holding burning charcoal to heat their homes. I'm sure we odd Americans were a source of amusement to the Japanese. The Emperor told his people to accept us and they did. There was never any show of resentment.

It is through the love of your Son, that we are shown how to love our former enemies. He said as He was nailed to the cross that dreadful day, "Father, forgive them." Let me be a peace maker.

The Japanese people were known for their ability to copy anything. My dad took in his favorite shirt to the tailor and asked for one just like it to be made in several colors. When he picked them up, they were truly a carbon copy of the one he provided the tailor. Unfortunately, he had dropped a cigarette ash on the flap of the pocket, so all four of the new shirts he picked up that day had the same cigarette burn on the flap as the original.

For the decades after the war "Made in Japan" meant to the buyer that the item in question was cheaply made. Decades later the manufacture of cars and electronics changed that perception from "cheap junk" to "quality."

Japan is now our strongest ally in the Far East. Time heals the wounds of the past. I still think about Kimiko Shimizu, our nanny. I hope she has had a wonderful rewarding life.

> **Trivia**: General Douglas MacArthur's father, Arthur MacArthur, was a Medal of Honor winner in the Civil War. Douglas was a West Point graduate and won seven Silver Stars in World War I. His flamboyant, non-regulation uniforms, and outlandish scene stealing mannerisms did not make him a favorite with his superiors. General "Black Jack" Pershing was very open about his dislike of MacArthur. General Douglas MacArthur was unashamedly a mama's boy. His mother, Pinky MacArthur, was given credit for her many military and civilian connections to lobby her son's promotion to brigadier general without the recommendation of his commanding officers. She remained the most powerful person in his life until his second marriage at age fifty-seven.

A Real Cup of Tea

Be of the same mind one toward another. Mind not high things, but condescend to men of low estate. Be not wise in your own conceits.   Romans 12:16

    My sister was just back from teaching math on a U.S. Navy ship stationed in Japan for two months. We met for lunch and then a little shopping. When we entered one of my favorite places to browse, a second-hand store run by a local charitable organization in Lewisville, Texas. Displayed near the cash register was a colorful red and blue Oriental plate. No, it couldn't be. Yes, it was. It was Imari. As I picked it up I heard my sister's voice say, "Are you interested in that?" If she hadn't of blinked, I'd be asking her if she was interested in that plate. "Yes," I said as I turned it over for her to inspect the Imari trademark.

    Ceramics have flourished in the Japanese culture since 10,000 BC. The venerated ceremonial tea ceremony, introduced in the 15th century, prompted the importing of Chinese porcelain. Chinese tea sets were considered works of art. Economic advances in the *Momoyama* period (1573-1615) resulted in the formation of a local manufacturing industry to compete with their Chinese rivals. After the Japanese invaded the Korean peninsula in 1592 and 1598, skilled Korean potters, who had been trained by the Chinese, were forcibly relocated to Japan. One of the talented Korean potters was a man named Ri Sampei. Ri Sampei is considered the "father" of Japanese porcelain.

    Japan was isolated from the rest of the world by order of the imperial family, the ruling shogun, and the samurai ruling class until the mid-19th century. When Admiral Matthew Perry made his visit in 1868, the Tokugawa shogun and his contingent of samurai wanted to remain an unchanged feudal kingdom. Lower-ranking samurai, who wanted to modernize the nation, challenged their rule. By 1870 the Emperor remained the divine leader of the Japanese people; however, laws establishing legal equality ended the samurai period of Japanese history.

We are taught to love one another as we love ourselves. More of our daily decisions should be made remembering we are all equal in the eyes of the Lord. The Good Book says to treat others as we would like to be treated. Help me make this part of my every day life.

Their only contact prior to the American Admiral Perry's forced open trade policy of 1868 was a few Dutch trading companies. The Dutch East India Company bought porcelain from the Arita kiln area of Sago Prefecture, the port of Imari. The rise of Japanese Imari resulted from the fall of the Ming Dynasty of China. The Dutch could no longer export the popular porcelain trade. When the Chinese porcelain trade resumed, they copied the Japanese.

Imari refers to porcelain produced with an underglaze of blue and overglaze polychrome enamel of gold, blue, red or rust, with gilded highlights. Items made for the Japanese market are blue and white. The themes reflect both Asian and European tastes. Chrysanthemums are the flower of choice for the Japanese version as it appears in the crest of the Imperial Japanese family. Thickness is another clue as to origin as the Chinese version was potted thinner. It also has a more evenly applied glaze.

Pieces from the earlier periods sell for hundreds and, sometimes, thousands of dollars. The Fukagawa family is known as the finest producers of all Arita. The modern company was founded by Chuji Fukagawa in 1894. He chose Mount Fuji and a stream beneath it as their trade mark.

The plate I bought in the photo is not a Fukagawa Imari plate, but I love it and it only cost the buyer, me, $4.50. I'm a happy shopper.

> **Trivia**: A samurai's income was based on the economic core of Japanese culture, rice. Rice was measured in a koku. A koku was 5 bushels of rice, the amount considered sufficient to feed one person for a year. The value of land was based on its rice producing qualities. High ranking samurai held fertile rice producing land. Lower ranking samurai were paid in rice and held no land.

The Innocence of a Child

And they brought young children to him, that he should touch them: and his disciples rebuked those that brought them. But when Jesus saw it, he was much displeased, and said unto them, Suffer the little children to come unto me, and forbid them not; for of such is the kingdom of God.
Mark 10:13-14

Mom reminded my dad as he left for the air base, "Don't bring me back any of those little kid figurines. They're just something else for me to dust." So he didn't.

Dad flew in the Berlin Airlift after World War II ended and those little inexpensive figurines all the GIs brought home were called Hummels.

Berta Hummel born in 1909 in rural Massing, Bavaria, Germany, drew the original pictures of her childhood friends as part of her education at the Academy of Fine Arts in Munich. Over four hundred works were completed during 1927-1931 when she graduated from the state school. Her professors and fellow students were surprised when she entered the Franciscan Convent of Siessen and took the name, Sister Maria Innocentia.

The first Hummel book of her drawings was published in 1934. That same year W. Goebel announced the start of production of the under 4" tall figurines. Forty-six figurines were ready for the Leipzig Spring Trade Show in 1935. Sister Innocentia dreaded the commercialization of her art; however, the National Socialist (Nazi) Party had taken over Germany and closed the convent's schools. The schools were the main source of income for the nuns. The Nazi government allowed the continued manufacture of the pieces for export only during the war years. The income from the sale of Hummels allowed the holy sisters to survive the five years of Nazi occupation of their beloved convent during World War II.

Sister Innocentia died of tuberculosis in November of 1946. We are still blessed with her remarkable talent.

Whether it's Michelangelo Buonarroti's the Creation of Adam on the Sistine Chapel or the art of a little known nun in Germany, we have visual reminders of God's love for mankind. Sister Maria Innocentia's ability to capture the innocence of a child is a timeless gift she continues to share with the world. Bless the little children.

There is no guessing, all Hummels are clearly marked. Refer to Goebel's chart of trademarks on www.antique-marks.com/hummel-marks.html. The symbols have changed many times in the last seventy years, but every piece should contain the signature of Sister M. I. Hummel (Maria Innocentia) and her stamp of approval. On the underside of the figure are the cipher for model number and year of release. Goebel is there in many different forms. A bee in tribute to Berta Hummel adorns most years. Another way to date them is if the trademark says W. Germany (West Germany) that would be the Cold War Years, from the end of WWII to the tearing down of the Berlin Wall.

Copies "in the style" of Hummel have flooded the market from China. They are easy to spot. There is very little detail and the paint is a poor imitation of the original.

If you plan to buy on ebay.com check the cost of mailing. One item I saw was very reasonable (under $50.00), but the mailing was $22.50, and that was from the U.S. Factor that into the figurine's price, mailing insurance, and you may have spent more than you intended. To find a retailer in your area go to www.mihummel.com.

Hint: To Clean - Hummels are made of earthenware. The interior is not glazed. Don't ever submerge them in water. Moisture on the inside will result in the paint on the outside fading. Each base's underside has an air hole to let out gases when the statue is fired. Seal the hole in the base before cleaning. Use a soft makeup brush dipped in baby shampoo and water to clean the statue. Wipe off with a clean wet soft towel.

As Time Goes By

For ye have need of patience, that, after ye have done the will of God, ye might receive the promise. Hebrews 10:36

My dad was home from the Berlin Airlift. His rhythmic snoring flowed down the hallway. That's not what woke me. I could sleep through that unless he did that snorting thing. I crawled up the ladder to my sister's bunk.

She didn't even open an eye as she muttered, "Get back in your own bed."

"But it scared me." I whined like a little sister would.

"You better get used to it." She rolled over and pushed me with her feet flinging me to the floor. "Get in your own bunk or I'll call Mom and tell her you're bugging me."

I crawled back into my bed and pulled the covers under my chin. My eyes refused to close. How long until that obnoxious bird cuckooed again?

Dad beamed when he handed Mom that handmade original Black Forest, five leaf, eight-day, cuckoo clock that chimed on the hour and half hour. Chimed is a kinder word than the sound that emitted from the wooden contraption with the pendulum that swung back and forth, and heavy pine cones that went up and down. It made a metal on metal clicking sound and then the bird barked out a "chirp" for each hour. Trust me it was not a pleasant calming song.

Mom and Dad said, "You'll get used to it and sleep right through the night."

When? I thought. "Maybe by the time I'm a hundred," I muttered to myself in the dark.

The hours and minutes of each day drive our lives. Sometimes our days are so hectic we forget to take time for ourselves. Time to recharge our inner self by speaking with the Father. Help us each day to remember that we can speak to You whenever the need arises. You are always there.

In 2000 BC Sumerians created the sexagesimal system of time measurement used still today to divide the hours and minutes of the day. Egyptians divided the day into two 12-hour periods and built obelisks to track the sun. Their shadow clocks relied on the sun's rays and were not reliable on cloudy days or inclement weather. The largest sundial ever built was in Rome during the reign of Emperor Augustus. Plato introduced water clocks in Greece in 500 B.C. Each century brought new ideas on how to measure time accurately.

It was not until late 996 A.D. that German monks further developed a mechanical timepiece based on the Arabic idea of weight driven mechanisms. This is the grandfather of our ever changing means of computing time. Prior to the Industrial Revolution, clocks were hand made so only wealthy patrons could afford them for their homes. Mass production brought affordable timepieces to the middle class.

Early America makers imported the brass workings of the clock from England and used native wood for the exterior. These timepieces became a piece of furniture. Tall case clocks (grandfather) and mantel (shelf) clocks were works of art.

The preeminent American clockmaker of the time was the Willard family of Massachusetts. Benjamin Willard started the company at his North Grafton workshop in 1766. When the demand required more production, he brought in his brothers, Simon, Ephraim, and Aaron. Simon Willard's masterpieces are the most sought after by collectors. At the encouragement of Thomas Jefferson, Simon patented his innovative "banjo" clock in 1802. It's considered the most significant style of nineteenth century American clocks.

Jones & Horan Auction Team, sold a tall clock made by Simon and Aaron Willard's apprentice, Daniel Munroe for

$54,000. Daniel established a short lived company with his two brothers in Concord, Massachusetts, from 1798-1804. Daniel and Nathaniel were clockmakers and their brother William made the beautiful Federal cabinets. Although many are unsigned, some contain verification on the dial face in a flowing style of penmanship, "D. Munroe & Co." In 2011 a Daniel Munroe diamond shaped-head banjo shelf clock circa 1804 was available on ebay.com for $45,500.

Granted the first patent for a clock mechanism in the United States, Eli Terry, inventor and clockmaker, changed the way the industry manufactured timepieces. At the time he entered the industry a skilled craftsman finished six to ten clocks per year. Terry bought a grain mill and used the water wheel technology to run saws and lathes to produce his mechanical parts. In three years time he was producing 3,000 clocks per year. Unlike his competitors, his clocks contained wooden mechanisms he produced en masse locally. This brought down the costs. His works still sell for thousands of dollars at auction. His son, Eli Terry Jr., excelled in the business and continued to produce premier examples of mid-19th century time pieces. Buyers must be aware that there are many reproductions on the market.

After working for Eli Terry for three years, Seth Thomas bought the Terry's factory. Thomas knew that for him to be successful he would have to be more diversified and self sufficient. He purchased a metal fabrication mill to provide his own movements and cases. He was later succeeded by his three sons, Seth Thomas Jr., Aaron, and Edward. The brothers introduced the first spring-driven clocks. Seth Thomas stamped their clocks on the base from 1880 to 1920. They also dated their clocks by code. Ex. 1908 became 8091 followed by a letter A for January thru L for December.

During 1903 William E. Sessions and family members purchased E.N. Welch Company. Sessions' father had produced cases for the faltering Welch Clock Company. Sessions Clock Company took off and never looked back. Sessions remained a major manufacturer until 1969 when it was sold. Early Sessions are favorites of collectors. They are beautiful, well-made, and affordable.

Trivia: As a fan of Pawn Stars on the History Channel, it never ceases to amaze me at the items people bring in to pawn or sell. On a March 2010 show a man brought in a small portable sun dial his father had gotten in Germany during the war. He wanted to pawn it for $500. Engraved on the case was "1662." Rick needed to call in an expert. His expert related it was a Nuremberg dial with several functions, including a weather vane, and in excellent condition. Its value was easily $7,000. Rick bought it for $4,500.

Cut Glass or Pressed That Is the Question

I will praise thee; for I am fearfully and wonderfully made: marvelous are thy works; and that my soul knoweth right well. Psalm 139:14

How many pioneer women packed their prize castor sets, compotes, or vases for the trip west, only to have to leave them along the trail to lighten the load? The Oregon Trail was littered with the belongings of these early travelers. What kept them going was their faith in God and their dreams. He would provide. He said so.

No sacrifice was too big for the sake of a woman's family and the quest for a better life for her children. It was back to basics for our forefathers and mothers. The comforts of her home would not include the elegant wedding gifts packed in her hope chest, which now rested on the shore of an unnamed stream in Wyoming. Her children would reap the harvest of their ventures.

My parents made sacrifices I did not realize until years later. There was no money to buy my prom dresses, yet they did. My sister and I needed expensive shoes to play varsity basketball. They bought us each a pair for four years. They did it to allow me to become the person I am today. I know now I don't need a new coat, when my neighbor has none. Children in America should not go to bed hungry. Guide me to be of service to others.

Spending the day walking through antique stores is still a kick for me even if I don't have any money to spend. One area that demands my attention every trip is the cut and pressed glass display. I am drawn to the area by how the light reflects from the different shades of transparent forms.

Years ago my mom brought me a celery vase she'd wrapped in a towel and carried in her luggage on the plane. In the late 1800's a mother would place a celery vase on the table with a little bit of water in the bottom and sticks of celery for snacking before the mealtime.

I hated to admit I couldn't tell cut glass from pressed glass. My research concluded the following information.

Cut glass gets its name from the fact that a rotating wheel cuts into a hand-held solid glass object to create the beautiful pattern we see. Run your finger over the outside of a piece of cut glass and you will feel the sharp edges of the facets cut out by the wheel. The facets catch and reflect the light just like a fine gemstone. The piece may be crystal clear or colored and is heavy because of the thick glass used.

This type of manufacturing was very labor intensive and thus expensive. It was not within the financial reach of the growing middle class. Glass makers of the 1800's found a quicker and more affordable way to fill that gap. Mass produced pressed glass filled the void with affordable ease.

American John P. Bakewell is credited with inventing the process in 1825 to make knobs for furniture. Molten glass is blown into a plain or engraved mold and then pressed into the sides with a plunger to create the pattern. It is the blunt edged facets and raised mold lines that identify pressed glass from cut glass. Now, run your finger around a piece of pressed glass. See the difference? The rounded facets are a dead give away it's not cut. Inspect the inside and bottom of the item and you will find the amount of seams vary from one to as many as four seams for bowls. Quality manufacturers smoothed mold marks so they would not stand out and the piece would better imitate the more expensive cut glass.

You may see ads with the caption "The American Brilliant Period." ABP lasted from 1850 to the early 1900's. Immigrant cutters brought their skills with them allowing American glass producers to compete with European. During this period the patterns became less intricate and less time consuming permitting more of them to be manufactured.

Another way to investigate your piece is to determine the pattern. This is not an easy matter as pressed glass was popular from 1825 until the Depression. When many manufacturers went out of business, they sold their molds to other companies that continued to produce the design. Before you spend your hard earned money, visit your public library and see if they carry any books on pressed and cut glass patterns. Look at pictures on the Internet. Go to an antique store and browse their wares. When you think you have something narrowed down, visit a bookseller, and purchase a book to further educate yourself. Visit websites like ebay.com to see what your pattern is bringing.

Don't buy off the Internet. To buy glass you have to be able to touch it. Feel for chips. Look for mold seams. Is the color right? These are all important questions that can't be answered by looking at a photograph.

Naturally, cut glass has more monetary value then pressed glass. A cut glass vase may sell for $100.00 and a pressed glass vase may be $10.00. Once again we must remember the law of supply and demand. Few families could afford cut glass so fewer items were produced thus making a smaller number available a hundred years later.

Cut glass is still a treasured gift. Names like Waterford (Ireland) and Baccarat (France) still mean elegance.

> **Hint**: Wash the glass pieces in ammonia. I use Parsons. Don't rinse, set it on a paper towel or dry with a tea towel. Set them on 12"H x 12"W mirror tiles you can get at Lowe's to display. The luminous tiles emit the light upward so the facets can catch and blush with the light.

There Is Beauty in the Midst of Despair

But when thou makest a feast, call the poor, the maimed, the lame, the blind: And thou shalt be blessed; for they cannot recompense thee: for thou shalt be recompensed at the resurrection of the just   Luke 14:13-14

    My mom fried the best chicken you have ever eaten. She made it light and crispy without being greasy. The thigh has always been my favorite part. Thank goodness there are two, because it was her favorite piece too. Whenever I visited she fried us both two thighs each, and made mashed potatoes and milk gravy. Colonel Sanders could have taken lessons from my mom. It really surprised me the evening she told me it had taken her years after she left home before she could eat chicken again.

    Today, when we see old movies about the 1920's era, the themes are about flappers, partying, gangsters and prohibition. Audiences of that period chose to see stories about glamorous debutantes and rich playboys or how a poor boy made good. These films aided in escaping the realities of their daily lives. Hard work and desperation consumed many of their waking hours.

    My grandfather was an Oklahoma wildcatter. He worked the oil rigs to support his family. Mom loved going to work with her dad. She has fond memories of her and her little brother chasing rabbits through the rows of pipes lined up to be buried in the red dirt of Oklahoma to transport the black gold elsewhere. She loved her dad and his easy going ways.

    In 1926 he died of pneumonia. Mom's mother was a 25 years-old widow with a third grade education. Her father had taken her out of school to pick cotton when her mother died in childbirth. Grandma had three children under the age of seven. There were no jobs. People stood in lines to eat at food kitchens.

    Blessed with in-laws that took them all in to live, they moved onto the farm Granddad's father claimed in the Oklahoma Cherokee Land Rush. The work was hard even for the youngest child. There was very little cash so they bartered for what they didn't grow. Chickens were a staple. Sunday dinner and several nights a week the family ate chicken. Mom learned as a six-year-old to kill, pluck, and fry chicken, or make chicken and dumplings or chicken pot pie. No wonder she got tired of the feathered fowl I so love.

Bless you for providing us with the spiritual food we need to reach our heavenly home. Thank you for providing the nourishment required to maintain our earthly bodies. When times are hard, true Christians answer the call and assist their brothers without a thought of "what's in it for me?" It's a simple answer. You will sit at the right hand of the Father.

Grandma made their clothes from flour sacks. Inside the flour was a beautiful glass cake plate or other dish in hues of pink, red, green, blue, cobalt, yellow, white, crystal, or amber. Boxes of soap powder may have contained tumblers or creamers. Merchants gave dishes out as premiums for trading at their store. You could even buy the etched pieces at Woolworth's Five and Dime store.

The first manufacturer of the machine produced depression era glassware was Indiana Glass Company in 1923. Within two years two dozen patterns were being produced mainly by: U.S. Glass Company, Imperial Glass Company, Jeanette Glass Company, Federal Glass Company, MacBeth-Evans, Hazel Atlas Glass, and Hocking Glass. Hocking merged with another company and became Anchor Hocking in 1937.

Early patterns were mass produced versions of the hand finished expensive glassware of this period called Elegant Glass, which only the wealthy could afford. The original 92 patterns are referred to as "known" patterns. There were also many additional pieces produced in unnamed "generic glass" patterns. Etched designs were produced by applying a thick coat of wax to the item. Secondly, a pattern was cut into the wax. Lastly, an acid was applied that couldn't penetrate the wax. The acid ate into the glass and created the recessed design. Hocking and others used a more common raised etching process by applying the wax and the acid process to the mold. This left the piece with a raised pattern.

Demand for the glassware dwindled as the public's taste changed and the onslaught of WWII required the raw materials for the war industry.

Glass prices depend on color, pattern, and availability. Stay away from chipped or damaged pieces. It just takes a moment to run your finger around the edges. Before buying, educate yourself. Pick up a copy of "Kovels' Depression Glass & Dinnerware Pricelist" or investigate the many websites devoted to depression era glass.

> **Trivia**: As the country left the Roaring Twenties and moved into a new decade, the 1930's, the economy continued to plunge into a deeper abyss. Imperial Glass Company filed for bankruptcy. Quaker Oats Company came to their rescue with an order for five boxcars of glassware to be used as premiums. Imperial designed the *No. 160 Cape Cod* pattern for them, which ended up being Imperial's best seller. This transaction was a major win-win for both companies.

The Potter's Hands

The word which came to Jeremiah from the Lord, saying arise, and go down to the potter's house, and there I will cause thee to hear my words. Then I went down to the potter's house, and, behold, he wrought a work on the wheels. And the vessel that he made of clay was marred in the hand of the potter: so he made it again another vessel, as seemed good to the potter to make it. Then the word of the Lord came to me saying, O house of Israel, cannot I do with you as this potter? saith the Lord. Behold, as the clay is in the potter's hand, so are ye in mine hand, O house of Israel.   Jeremiah 18:1-6

As you drove eastbound across the I-94 bridge that separated Minnesota and Wisconsin, you could see our quaint little white house with the black trim and red door perched on the side of the hill. You had to venture up three flights of stairs to reach the entry. Originally built in the 1940's it functioned as the owner's weekend cabin. Now, after several decades, two additions, and lots of love, it was our blessed escape from the busy Twin Cities. Our home. Our refuge.

The most valuable asset of our abode could be seen from every window on the west side of the residence. The beautiful St. Croix River slowly meandered past on its way to Hastings to join the Mississippi River on its journey to New Orleans. Each evening in the spring and summer a parade of boats and a flotilla of hot air balloons filled our minds with wanderlust; an itch to join them in their carefree adventure.

Along both the Minnesota and Wisconsin shorelines the small "river towns", as locals call them, invite strangers to stop and stay awhile. They are historic entities of their own. In the mid-1800's lumber jacks filled the St. Croix with trees they'd logged up river, and then rode them on the current to the towns downstream. The Mississippi and St. Croix Rivers were the roads of their time and today barges still travel the Mississippi.

Thank you for giving us these moments to remember. Life is not about a bank balance or who has the most toys. Life is about relationships with You, our families, and with nature. Help me remember what is really important and what is not. Make me a better decision maker.

Come the weekend, I filled a cooler with two days of food, water, and soft drinks and we headed for the door. Our yacht, a 24' hard-top convertible cruiser, awaited us at the dock. It only took a few minutes to leave the no-wake zone and then enter the main stream current to ride south. Thank goodness, power boats and jet skis preferred the lakes to the slow pace of the river. Fellow boaters smiled and waved as we drifted past. There was no hurry. We relaxed and took in the beautiful scenery.

Once through the lock and dam, there was only twenty miles until we reached our destination. My husband parked the boat at the charming Red Wing City Park dock. The convenient landing enticed boaters to stop and shop. A craft fair was in progress in the park. We purchased gifts for the grandchildren then proceeded into town to visit the real reason we came down the river that day. Red Wing, Minnesota is the home of both Red Wing Shoes and Red Wing Pottery.

Red Wing Stoneware crocks, pitchers, mugs, jugs, and other products are highly collectible. In every area of our nation there was a regional pottery company that supplied products to the surrounding area. Because of the Mississippi River and the availability of clay, David Hallem started Red Wing Stoneware Co. in 1868.

What is stoneware? It was in early kitchens because of its durability. Unlike earthenware that is made from a low-fired clay, stoneware is created from a high fired clay. This makes it sturdy enough for cooking, baking, and preserving liquids. That crock that great-grandma used to make pickles or sauerkraut was most likely stoneware. You can tell it's stoneware by the weight. It was made dense for durability. Buff was the usual color. Early pieces were hand thrown. As the industry grew molds were introduced.

As stoneware lost favor with the buying public at the turn of the 20th Century, Red Wing Potteries started its manufacturing of art pottery and dinnerware. After closing in 1967, the stoneware production was revitalized in 1984. The current owner continues the traditions of his predecessors in providing a quality product at reasonable prices. You can view their factory and gift shop at www.redwingstoneware.com.

The logo has changed many times over the years. The Red Wing stamp and classic cobalt blue design appear in each version.

Trivia: A trip to Minnesota would not be complete without visiting the headwaters of the great Mississippi River. Itasca State Park, near Bemidji, is home to the most incredible sight. The source of the longest river in our nation is a place you can step across. You have to see it to believe it. While in the area visit the famous lumberjack, Paul Bunyan, and his famous sidekick, Babe, The Blue Ox.

Grandma's Gift

God loves a cheerful giver.   2 Corinthians 9:7

In the past we Americans never threw anything away. Mothers would just "move it" up to the attic, while dads would "find a spot for it" in the basement. There it would sit until needed or discovered by a curious child.

My daughter, Trish, was about 4 years-old when my mother-in-law took her upstairs to explore their attic. It was hot, dark, and stuffy. You could barely make out boxes of Christmas decorations and books in one direction and a couple old suitcases in the other. Along the back wall Grandpa Baumker built several rows of shelves for Grandma to store her miscellaneous items.

Grandma Baumker reached up and pulled the string to turn on the overhead light. Trish marveled at the objects that came alive. A female manikin held out her arms as if modeling the partially completed dress that adorned her form. Toys that had been her Dad's still covered the floor. Tonka trucks and trains left out by her boy cousins that had visited the month before. A painting easel sat near the window to capture the best light.

Grandma walked towards the shelves. She pointed at two tea pots. "Take the one you want." Trish picked the brown one and carried it downstairs.

"Thank you." She remembered to say as she hugged Grandma and headed to the kitchen to show us her prize.

I wrapped it carefully so it wouldn't chip on our trip home.

Everyone has those moments in our lives when we relive a cherished moment with those who have passed on. We keep our loved ones alive in our memories and the knowledge that we will see them again when we join You in heaven. Let me be a person that has formed lasting friendships. Let me be there when needed.

Two weeks later after dinner with my parents, I told Mom about the trip to Ohio and mentioned Trish's tea pot. "Let me see it," she requested. I retrieved it, unwrapped it, and gave it to Mom to examine. "It's a Weller," she said.

Puzzled, I asked, "What's a Weller?" "Weller was one of the best art potteries in Ohio. It's very collectible. This teapot is a great example of their work."

American art pottery came into vogue in the 1870s. Crafted from the same clay used in stoneware, it was a line of products that potteries produced for its aesthetic as well as utilitarian purpose. Most of the items prized by collectors today came from an area near Zanesville, Ohio. The quality of the local clay and ease of shipping on adjoining rivers produced successful potters such as the top three companies of Weller, Rookwood, and Roseville.

Samuel Weller started the Weller Pottery Company in 1872 in a small cabin in Fultonham, Ohio, to take advantage of the Muskingham County clay. In Fultonham he produced simple household items such as jars and jugs for the local farmers and small villages in the area. In 1882 Sam moved to Zanesville where he branched out from functional everyday earthenware items to become a highly stylized art manufacturer with 200 employees. He hired artists to produce designs and glazes that became wildly popular with the buying public. His ability to change with the tastes of his customer is reflected in his pieces being referred to as Art Nouveau, Arts and Crafts Movement, and Art Deco styles. Unable to compete with the influx of cheap imports after WWII, the company closed. Weller Pottery remains very collectible and affordable.

It's estimated that Weller Pottery had 125 different product lines. Their trademarks varied from the easily identifiable to a specialized mark. A good resource would be *Warman's Weller Pottery: Identification and Price Guide, Kovels' Dictionary of Marks: Pottery and Porcelain: 1650 to 1850 or Pictorial Guide to Pottery and Porcelain Marks* by Chad Lage, November 1, 2003. There are also so many internet sites that specialize in Weller.

Rookwood Pottery in Cincinnati started as the hobby of wealthy women's club member, Mrs. Maria Longworth Nichols Storer. Impressed by the display of Japanese ceramics at the Philadelphia Centennial in 1876, Mrs. Storer, an amateur china painter, went on to study the manufacture and firing of pottery. Her father bought her a shop, a former schoolhouse, and a kiln in 1880. Early pots displayed Asian themes. W. W. Taylor joined Mrs. Storer in 1883. He then went on to take control of the pottery in 1883. He built a new facility in Cincinnati in 1889. Mrs. Storer recruited artists from the Cincinnati Art School to continue the characteristic Rookwood style. They developed new types of glazing and methods of firing decorations and glazing. Since pieces were hand-decorated each piece is unique.

Rookwood has a distinctive marking system: body or clay mark, size mark, date mark, decorator mark, and factory mark. Antiques Roadshow made America aware of the beauty and quality of Rookwood. Prices rose accordingly. There were very few fakes made.

The third Ohio outstanding pottery company was of course Roseville Pottery. Roseville is probably the most recognizable of the Ohio pottery companies.

Roseville, Ohio, was home to the pottery that would take its name. Opened by a team of investors in the late 1880s, by 1910 all administration and production had relocated to Zanesville. Rookwood Standard Glaze Ware was their biggest competitor. Roseville Pottery hired Ross Purdy in 1900 to create a line of art ware, which they named Rozane. Like Rookwood, the Rozane line was hand decorated and signed. In 1904 Frederick Rhead came on board as art director and developed a strong commercial line. Under his leadership many of the pieces sought by today's collectors were produced. The most coveted are pieces from the 1920's to 1930's. Art Director Frank Ferrell produced the most successful line of the company, Pinecone.

After WWII the company attempted new lines to revive the waning interest in earthenware, but to no avail. Like its competitors, Roseville ceased production in 1954 when it was bought by the Mosaic Tile Co.

Buyer beware. There are many Roseville fakes. Pieces should be marked Roseville and Roseville USA. Many fakes are marked similarly. The type glaze used separates the real from the fake. Study the books available and on the internet to be confident you are buying the real thing.

Those mentioned above are the three American Art Pottery producers most in demand in today's market. Many other noteworthy companies include McCoy, Hull, and Frankoma. They continue to be available at reasonable prices.

Trivia: This restaurant review is one of the choices you get when you google Rookwood. The old Rookwood factory is now a restaurant. You can dine in a kiln if you have a reservation. Think of the ambiance. Reviewers suggest you order the Barnsdale Burger.

"Atmosphere - FIVE STARS - This place is the old Rookwood pottery with kilns, exposed brick, and a very unique atmosphere. You can dine in a kiln with reservations. We sat in one by the bar while we were waiting for the rest of our party, and it was pretty neat. Also, when they pour you your water at the table, they use the old Bulliet Bourbon bottles to pour the water in your glass...really cool touch. We didn't go outside, but their deck setup looks to be probably the best in the city."

You're A Doll

Lo, children are a heritage of the Lord: and the fruit of the womb is His reward. As arrows are in the hand of a mighty man; so are children of the youth. Happy is the man that hath his quiver full of them. Psalm 127:3-5

When Clara was born in New York City in 1899, life was hard for the second generation immigrant family. She must have been thrilled the day her parents presented her with a beautiful imported bisque doll from Germany. Most little girls only had rag dolls, or dolls whose head and shoulders were bisque, but their bodies were cloth. No, Clara's baby had a five piece composition body. She helped it wave bye, bye. Her baby doll had puckered red lips and pink cheeks. They were the focal points of the round light-skinned face. Her azure glass eyes opened and closed as Clara laid her to rest and then picked her up and hugged her close. A wig of soft blond curls topped the child-like body dressed in an ivory lace dress. Any little girl would love and treasure this baby doll.

So how did Clara's doll end up with one of her brothers seventy years later? We'll never know. He used it outside in the cold and snowy Ohio winters as part of his Christmas display. Her once beautiful wig rested in complete disarray and made her look "scary" to the youngest family members. Her days of being held and adored were over.

When offered, we took her home with us.

Years later we were transferred from Louisiana to South Dakota. The movers came to pack our household goods. I mentioned that the life-sized antique doll required special packaging. I watched as the man took my floor pillows and threw them in a box. He picked up the doll and placed her on the pillows then put more floor pillows on top of her and continued to fill the box. All day I worried about her. When they left I opened the box. Across her forehead was a small hairline crack. There was nothing I could do. Since then I have packed my own antiques and moved them in my car. I can't fault the mover's personnel.

It was my responsibility to ensure she was properly wrapped and packed.

We need to take responsibility for our own actions. It's easier to say "it wasn't my fault." That little voice inside reminds us we should have known better. Help us make better decisions so we don't spend a lifetime of regret.

Homemade cloth, cornhusk, and wooden dolls remained prevalent until the 1850s. Those families wealthy enough to buy dolls bought imported ones for their little girls. France, with companies like Jumeau and Bru, stood as the foremost manufacturer. Germany, with Kammer & Reinhart and Simon & Halbig, approached at a close second.

German immigrants brought their knowledge to America and helped spark a new industry. Ludwig Greiner received the first patent in 1858. His patent covered his manufacturing of only the head and shoulders. Customers added the body, usually made from wood or cloth. American companies had a few successes. Kewpie dolls started as illustrations in a 1908 Ladies Home Journal. The original bisque dolls were made in Germany in 1912. Since that time they have been manufactured in celluloid, composition, and today they are in vinyl. One American manufacturer currently producing the Kewpie is Charisma Company, a Marie Osmond doll company.

In 1915 artist Johnny Gruelle received a patent for cloth dolls based on two characters from his children's books, Raggedy Ann and Raggedy Andy. The first Raggedy Ann had brown yarn hair, not red, and shoe button eyes and can bring $1,000.00 in today's market.

In 1977 the Cabbage Patch Kids, a cloth doll with a vinyl head, stole America's heart and caused chaos at retailers. Fifty-seven million Cabbage Patch Kids were adopted before their craze ended.

After WWI American companies experimented with new technologies. Rubber, celluloid, and plastics replaced the fragile bisque-head dolls. The "Big Four"- Mattel, Ideal, Horseman, and Madame Alexander rivaled their European competitors. The homegrown companies added a touch of inventiveness such as Dy-Dee Baby, a doll that drank and wet.

The 1950s ushered in a softer plastic, which allowed more awareness to detail. Ginnys, made by Vogue, and Tiny Tears by American Character, were manufactured in several sizes (heights) and with wardrobes to interest a new generation. Also, television characters left the small screen to play in children's toy boxes. Howdy Doody, Beanie and Cecil, Disney, and comic book characters were in high demand.

And the queen of dolls, Barbie, made her début on March 9, 1959. Named after creator Ruth Handler's daughter, Barbara, the original was introduced as an adult fashion model. Few dolls were sold until Mattel Toys started an advertising campaign on *The Mickey Mouse Club* television show. Barbie has since had 80 career changes, including astronaut and presidential candidate. There have been enough Barbie and Barbie family members sold to circle the earth seven times. This significant amount of product has not deterred the modern collector. Collector editions of Barbie are made in limited quantities of 35,000 dolls and are produced to be displayed rather than played with by the recipient. Blondes must have more fun as more blonde dolls have been sold making the early brunette and red-haired versions more desirable to collectors. Vintage collectors are looking for versions cataloged as #1 thru #6. The Internet has many sites dedicated to Mattel's diva for research. In addition to dolls, clothing and accessories have a large market.

There are several categories for doll collectors:
- Antique: 1800s to 1920s
- Vintage: 1930s to 1980s

- Modern: The last 25 years
- Contemporary: Made today

What collectors are looking for:
- Condition: No skin damage, neither blemishes nor dark spots, or only slight skin crazing. Clean-no dirt. Not restored.
- Maker: Company name, mold number, and dates, displayed on the back or hip of the body, across the shoulders, on a leg or arm, or at the base of the head. Later dolls still having their original tag.
- Size of doll and material used. Dolls are usually classified by the material their heads are made of: bisque, china, porcelain, rubber, hard plastic, vinyl, composite, corn stalk, etc. Size varies from very small to life-size.
- Rarity- Shirley Temple dolls in a complete original costume are hard to find.
- Appropriate costume: Garments like-new and never laundered.
- Hair: Original wig or eye lashes whether natural hair or mohair.

Terminology:
- A/O: All original
- Applied ears: The ears were molded separately from the remaining head and applied later.
- BéBé: French doll that represents small children.
- Ball jointed dolls (BJD): Dolls strung together that have small wooden balls in the joints at the neck, elbows, wrists, knees, ankles, and hips that allows the extremities to move as a real person's would.
- Bisque: Unglazed, flesh-tinted, matt-finish porcelain
- China: Glazed porcelain. A combination of kaolin clay and ground feldspar and additional additives. Very breakable.
- Celluloid: As mentioned earlier, an early plastic. Very combustible.
- Character doll: A doll that is patterned after a living person.

- Closed mouth: A doll whose lips are closed so no teeth show.
- Composition: A version of paper mache´. It consisted of sawdust and glue that was heated and poured into molds for doll heads and bodies.
- Crazing: Fine cracks.
- DEP: A term found on French and German antique dolls meaning patented.
- Dollhouse doll: Ranged in size from one inch to one foot to fit in a dollhouse.
- Domed head: The top of the head is closed.
- Fashion doll: A French or German doll with a bisque head that wears the clothing of the current period.
- Five piece body: A five piece body consists of a torso, two arms, and two legs.
- Flanged neck: Where the body of the doll is attached to the head.
- Flirty eyes: Eyes that move side to side.
- Googly-eyed: Made from 1912-1938, they were flirty eyed dolls whose faces were made from bisque or composition in a mask fashion and then adhered to a cloth body. The large "goo-goo" eyes, a trademark of Barney Google the cartoon character, gave the doll her nickname.
- Gusseted joint: A type of joint used in leather and cloth bodies.
- Gutta percha bodies: An early form of latex. Sap from the Isonandra Gutta tree that grew on the Malay Peninsula was used by the French doll industry to create heads and bodies in the nineteenth and twentieth centuries. It was easy to use, but expensive.
- Jointed body: See ball-jointed dolls above.
- Half-dolls: Adult dolls manufactured between 1915-1930, they were modeled themes for women not children. The torso extends to below the waist. Holes in this area allowed clothing to be attached. One factor in estimating the value of the piece is determined by how far away from the body the arms extended.

- Hard plastic: Type of material used between 1940 and 1950.
- Hairline: A crack in a bisque doll that can barely be seen.
- HTF: Hard to find.
- Intaglio eyes: Eyes that are molded into the doll's head to be painted during a later process.
- Inset eyes: Fixed in position and do not move. Common in pre-19th century dolls.
- Mark: Manufacturer's identification marks.
- MIB: Mint in box.
- MIP: Mint in package lets you know the accessories are intact.
- MNB: Mint condition doll, but not in original box.
- Mohair: Angora goat hair used in making doll wigs.
- Molded ears: Ears molded in the doll head; the opposite of applied ears.
- Mold number: The manufacturer's number that signifies the mold used to make the doll.
- NRFB: Never removed from box.
- OOAK- One of a kind.
- OSS: Doll is in the original swim suit.
- Open mouth: Doll's lips are open to see teeth inside.
- Open/closed mouth: Mouth molded to look open, however, there is no actual opening in the bisque.
- Open head: The crown is open to be able to insert the eyes later. A pate covers the spot.
- Parian: Unglazed and un-tinted porcelain.
- Pate: A piece of cardboard, cork, or other material that fills in the crown of an open head doll.
- Poupee: French fashion dolls.
- Provenance: The history of ownership of an antique doll.
- Presentation box: The original materials used by retailers to sell/display the doll. This may include the original box, furniture, clothing, and accessories.

- Reborn baby doll: A vinyl doll that is prepared to resemble a real baby as closely as possible. This is considered an art and can cost hundreds of dollars.
- Reproduction: Dolls created to look like antique dolls.
- Rubber: Patented by Charles Goodyear in 1844, vulcanized rubber's durability appealed to the post WWII doll market.
- Shoulder head doll: Only the shoulders and head are bisque. The remainder of the doll is of another material.
- Sleep eyes: Eyes that close when the doll is laid down and open when they are upright.
- Socket head: A cup and saucer type attachment holds the molded neck and head of the doll.
- Rocker bar eyes: The eyes are placed on a T-bar inside the head and clamped to the doll's head. A weight "rocks" the eyes closed as the doll is placed in a prone position and opens them as it is held upright.
- UFDC: United Federation of Doll Clubs.

Trivia: In 1830 Charles Goodyear had an India rubber manufacturing plant in Staten Island, New York. Here he produced maps, surgical bandages, and toys. The rubber manufactured had very little elasticity rendering it brittle in cold and a sticky mess in hot conditions. While he experimented at home by boiling rubber and sulfur in 1839, he dripped some of the brew on his wife's hot stove. It vulcanized giving the compound the ability to adjust to hot and cold temperatures. During the next twelve years after perfecting vulcanized rubber, Goodyear applied for a patent to make doll heads out of rubber. Rubber doll heads replaced the fragile bisque heads ones. Charles' Goodyear Rubber Company trade journal of 1881 contained three pages of doll heads. Never a good businessman, Goodyear even went to prison for a term, he died deeply in debt in 1860. In 1898 Frank Sieberling opened The Goodyear Rubber Company that we know today. Sieberling named it after Charles Goodyear as a sign of respect for his having invented the process used to produce tires.

Yes, I Can

Whether therefore ye eat, or drink, or whatsoever ye do, do all to the glory of God.   1 Corinthians 10:31

Okay, so this chapter is about canning jars. Don't flip to the next chapter. Mason jars can be creative, interesting, and profitable. Napoleon Bonaparte said "An army marches on its stomach." Napoleon put his money where his mouth was. Martha Stewart makes candle holders out of them. A woman bought one at a garage sale and sold it for $44,000.00. Now, it's getting more interesting isn't it?

Glass production goes back to Mesopotamia in the second and third millennium B.C. and traveled by caravan to Egypt and Phoenicia. In the first millennium B.C. along the Eastern Mediterranean glass blowing originated allowing access to the masses. As the Roman Empire spread so did the production of glass manufacturing. As the Empire waned so did the industry. It wasn't until about the 13th century that it experienced a rebirth in Venice.

War and malnutrition were both rampant during the 1700 and 1800's. During the Napoleonic Wars, General Bonaparte offered a reward of 12,000 francs to anyone who could provide his army and navy with portable wholesome food. It remained illusive until a pastry chef named Nicholas Appert established a procedure. His method enclosed fruits or vegetables in glass containers, sealing the contents with pitch and then boiling for a period of time. (Pitch – A resin derived from the sap of various coniferous trees. American Heritage College Dictionary, 3rd Edition) This hermetically sealed the contents. Within a short period of time other inventors patented the use of tin-coated iron cans, and tins of aluminum based on Appert's idea.

May we never take for granted the bounty You have provided. Let us never forget to praise You for Your love and generosity.

In America John Landis Mason invented and patented the common glass jar used to preserve food. Mason was a tinsmith by trade. His patent dated November 30, 1858, is primarily based on the use of exterior threads on the jar neck and a corresponding metal cap. This allowed the jars to be reusable and thus inexpensive for home canners to use.

When Mason's patent expired in 1879, several large companies started producing fruit-canning jars. The most notable is the Ball Glass Manufacturing Company. Their oldest jars go back to 1884, and were manufactured in Buffalo, New York. They are referred to as "Buffalo jars." BBGMCo was embossed on the bottom. A new plant opened in Muncie, Indiana, in 1888 and a whopping 41 million jars were manufactured there. It was this infusion of jars that kept collectors from scrambling to acquire Ball jars. Recently, this trend has changed. Many are accumulating samples of all the different logos Ball has used in the last 120 years.

You may refer to a canning jar by many names: Mason jar, Ball jar, fruit jar, and jam jar. They're all correct. Add to that Kerr, Atlas, Knox, Decker's Iowan, Corning, Mom's, and Presto. Available sizes range from half pint to a gallon, which makes my back hurt just thinking of lifting a filled container that size.

To decide the age of your jar start with determining if the item was done by a glassblower or blown into a mold. A pontil scar is a noticeable indentation that signifies a glassblower held the jar on a rod while it was still hot. These jars were made before 1855. Check for a mold seam. Early jars were blown without a mold. Later versions have mold seams to the lip. The neck and top were added by hand later. After 1915 the mold seam will reach to the top as machines were introduced to production. The patent date of November 30, 1858, was embossed on Mason jars until the 1920's. So this shouldn't be used to determine the age of the jar. You may turn the jar over and look for a run number on the bottom.

Color helps determine its value. Clear and aqua are considered colorless. Blues vary from light to cobalt. Milk glass, blacks, and cobalt are hard to find. Amber and yellow are easy to find. Greens from citron, a yellowish green, to emerald remain available. Our grandmothers didn't buy jars for the pretty colors. The tint had a purpose. It kept out the light, which helped retain the food's flavor and nutritional value. Forgeries continue to be made in many colors including cobalt, green, black, and olive green. Many have the mold number of 851 on the base. Even as reproductions they sell in the $50.00 range.

Collectors are looking for intact jars meaning the right lids. Earliest lids used sealing wax to hold the tin lid to the lip of the glass jar. During the Civil War the thumb screw clamp device, which consisted of metal wire clamps, held the glass lid and gasket in place. The Kline Stopper, also called a bail closure, followed. It used a gasket and glass stopper on the mouth of the heated jar. As the jar cooled the vacuum was created. Mason's screw on zinc cap replaced the use of wax, an often untrustworthy sealer, and the Kline Stopper. The Buffalo jars had glass lids with zinc bands. From 1860-1900 many types of closures were patented. Some were absurd. It is these rare items that draw the collector's attention and command the highest prices.

I made you wait long enough. A woman, who will remain nameless except to PayPal and the IRS, found a cathedral shaped pickle jar at a garage sale. She gladly paid the $3.00 and took it home. She placed it on ebay.com to sell. It sold for $44,100.00. Savvy collectors recognized it as one of only five cathedral shaped pickle jars known in the world.

My grandparents planted their Pennsylvania acreage with fruit trees and vines so their nine children, and many grandchildren, could fill their empty bellies. Each year my grandmother planted a garden of organic vegetables before "organic" became a method of growing vegetables.

Colorful jars of canned cherries, peaches, corn, and green beans stood in rows on the shelves in the larder off the kitchen. Everything tasted better when it came right from grandma's garden. I still find myself wondering when I get home from grocery shopping, what my grandfather would say if he knew what we pay for fresh fruits and vegetables.

During the 1980's and 90's, I canned pickles, and made applesauce and apple butter. Even with all the conveniences of today's kitchen, it was hard hot work. It makes you admire all the women that came before us. I did it for fun. They had to toil in the hot kitchen so their families could eat. How spoiled we have become. Gardens are not essential. They're a hobby.

Thanks for providing beyond our wildest dream. You only asks us to acknowledge where our blessings come from. That's not much to ask of us, His children. Recognition.

> **Trivia**: John Landis Mason, the inventor of the Mason jar, died a pauper in 1902.

I can't end this chapter without sharing this great recipe. Don't skip the ice cube treatment. This makes them crisp.

Bread and Butter Pickles

4 quarts sliced cucumbers
1 green pepper, sliced thin
1/3 Cup pickling salt
5 Cups sugar
1½ teaspoon celery seed
6 onions, sliced
3 garlic cloves
3 Cups white vinegar
1½ teaspoon turmeric
2 teaspoons mustard seed

Wash cucumbers, do not peel, slice them. Layer cucumbers with sliced onions, green pepper strips, and garlic cloves. Sprinkle with salt. Make additional layers. Mix in several trays of ice cubes and end up ice cubes on the top layer. Let stand 3 hours. Drain thoroughly. Place cucumbers in prepared canning jars. (I wash then put them in boiling water to sterilize for 10 minutes with the seals and lids.) Combine vinegar, sugar, and spices. Heat brine to boiling. Pour over cucumbers in jars. Seal. Place in canner or deep pan about 10 minutes. Let stand a month before eating.

Don't Fence Me In

He watereth the hills from his chambers: the earth is satisfied with the fruits of thy works. He causeth the grass to grow for the cattle, and herb for the service of man: that he may bring forth food out of earth.

Psalm 104:13-14

Like many kids born in the 1940's and 1950's, every Saturday we made our way to the local Bijou with quarters in hand to see a double feature and suck on a Sugar Daddy. The movies were usually two westerns accompanied by a serial and two cartoons. My favorite cowboy was Hopalong Cassidy. Hoppy's big white horse, Topper, was magnificent. George "Gabby" Hayes played many an actor's comic sidekick. Life seemed so simple then. Everything was black and white. At least in the black and white movies it was. How did life change so fast for the Old West? What killed the cowboy lifestyle?

During the long winter of 1872-1873, a young wife noticed her long wire hair pins kept disappearing from the dish on her dresser. Strange, who needed her hair pins? She questioned her daughter. "No," she wasn't using them. Then who? One evening after supper Lucinda Glidden noticed her husband reach into his pocket and take out two of the missing pins. "Joseph, what are you doing with my hairpins?" He replied he had an idea for a new type of wire fence.

In 1868, Michael Kelly created a double strand wire with a barb in the middle. It was referred to as a "thorny fence." It replaced the single strand version that cattle would lean against and knock down. When patented in November of 1874, Glidden's patent #157,124 fence was an improvement of Kelly's version. It is this style that continues in use today.

With the use of barbed wire, cattle herders were confined to the use of public lands. As the public lands dwindled, cattle herding became extinct. With the introduction of barb wire fencing nomadic Native

Americans could no longer follow the buffalo. They referred to the new wire as "the Devil's rope."

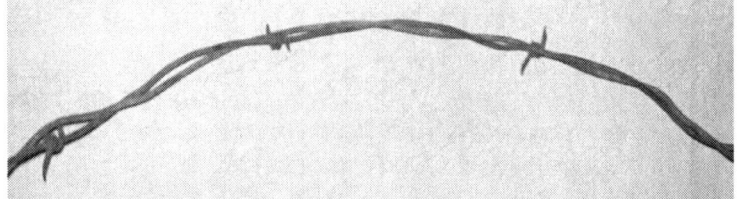

As our way of life adapts to circumstances often beyond our control, like the cowboys of old, You prepare the way for us. As one door closes another opens. Help me understand that what I want is not always what I need.

The most recognizable difference between samples are the type of barb, how many points protrude, the shape of the points, and how the barb is attached to the wire. Even raw stock wire bought from steel mills varied in size, shape, and ingredients. Wire made by small groups and blacksmiths was made to their own specifications to avoid patent infringement.

There are almost six hundred patents for barb wire and over two thousand variations of the wire that have been cataloged. Rare examples are the most collectable. Usually collectors are interested in specimens that are at least 18" in length. This shows the spacing between the barbs.

Other collectors want mounted displays of 4" to 6".

This version also contains a detailed description of the wire including:
- Name of the author of the ID book being used.
- Name of the wire and characteristics.
- Patent Number.
- Date of Issue.
- Patentee's name and location of their residence.

Trivia: One of the most famous cowboy songs ever, "Don't Fence Me In" was written by Cole Porter in 1934 for a 20th Century Fox movie musical, *Adios, Argentina*. The lyrics were based on a poem authored by Robert Fletcher, who worked for the Department of Highways in Helena, Montana. Porter bought the poem from Fletcher for $250.00. Ten years later Roy Rogers sang the song in the 1944 movie, *Hollywood Canteen*, but Bing Crosby and the Andrews Sisters made it a best-seller later that year.

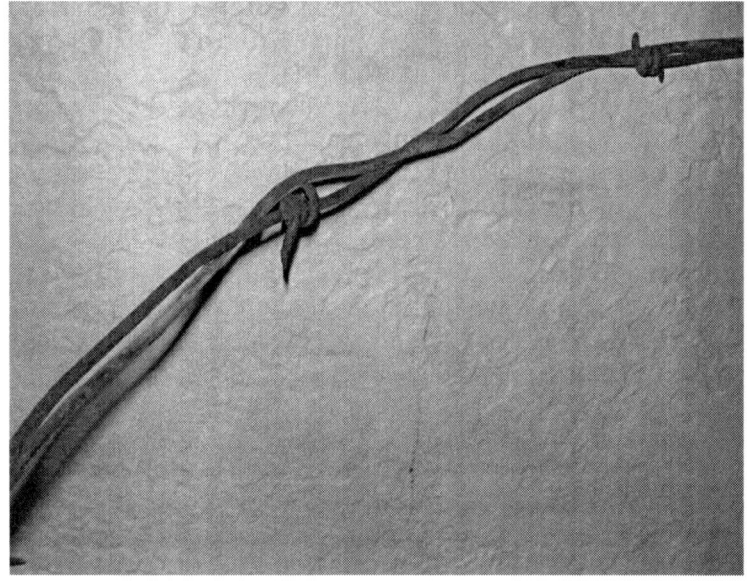

"Oh, give me land, lots of land under starry skies above, Don't fence me in..."

It Pays to Advertise

A merry heart doeth good like a medicine. Proverbs 17:22

I grew up in a time in our nation's history when my biggest decision of the week was what to wear on my date Saturday night. As most girls my age, I had my heart broken a couple of times. Either he didn't call or he called too often, which made my dad upset with me. That prompted Dad to set the egg timer with each call. I either hung-up or he would.

One boyfriend had "glass packs" on his cruiser. "Vroom. Vroom." This really raised my dad's blood pressure when "that loud car" turned into our driveway.

One day as Dad drove me to work the Marine recruiter's ad came on the radio. Dad laughed. "That's what you need to do, Tammy." He smiled an ornery grin at me. "What?" I replied having no idea where this conversation was going. "You need to call the Marines and have them make you a man."

"Funny, Dad." It still makes me grin when I think about that morning.

We need to have those moments with our parents that make us laugh, make us cry. Years later when we mature we are able to see them as mere mortals. God, our heavenly Father, provides our earthly family to teach us lessons we need to know to reach His kingdom. Make me a better teacher than I was a student.

Dad proved it pays to advertise. Any time you can get a listener/viewer to quote your advertisement or tell another person about it, you've reached your objective.

Advertising Part I — Antiques

We're not the first to get the word out by advertising. The first known civilization to communicate their wants and desires were the Sumerians in 3000 B.C. They etched pictograms into clay to form a language called cuneiforms. Egyptians followed with hieroglyphics and the first outside billboard. Alphabets and the printed word developed, and man was in the advertising business.

It may have been a handbill the American immigrant saw in Europe that prompted him to catch a boat to the New World. Handbills and newspapers were an early means of getting information out to the public. Promotions of goods-on-hand by retailers or the local craftsman were included. Ben Franklin was the first to include a woodcut image along with the printed word in his publications the *Philadelphia Gazette* and *Poor Richard's Almanac*. The invention of the high speed lithograph printing press resulted in the establishment of regional and national magazines. It also allowed color images. Newspapers flourished, but they failed to inform a large part of our population. Illiterate and citizens who spoke a language other than English, had to be reached to buy retailers' wares.

As early as 1300 A.D., iron was tinplated in Bohemia. Tinsmiths made crude, but durable and cheap household items. Tin cans were not made of tin. The term tin can was a shortened version of tinplated canister. Germany dominated the industry. In 1706 Britain passed a protective tariff against German tin ware. From that point her tin industry overshadowed European producers. American producers used the cheaper government protected British containers until the McKinley Tariff passed the U.S. Congress in 1891. This tariff allowed a level playing field for American tin manufacturers to thrive.

In 1800 a tinsmith could make 6 tins per hour by hand; by the end of the century machinery made 2500 per hour. As noted earlier the lithograph printer allowed the application of a colored image and lettering. This replaced hand painted or paper labels. Labels were necessary for the variety of foods canned. Urban and mobile populations increased the demand for fruits and vegetables in convenient containers. New canning processes made the food more palatable.

America in the 1800s was ready for new ideas. During this period store chains appeared. Traditional general stores became specialized. Premiums such as mirrors, calendars, paperweights, metal trays, and trade cards drew customers to their retail stores. Not only national brands, but local community brands joined production of promotional merchandise.

By the mid to late 1800's product recognition by the use of images, rather than just wordage, was firmly established. Advertisement agencies formed to meet the needs of national advertisers. They designed artwork and verbiage to attract buyers' attention.

John S. Pemberton, the inventor of Coca-Cola, understood that national promotion of his product would further establish his new company. Founded in 1886, that first year the company spent more money on marketing than the business made in sales. Pemberton deemed this an investment in the Coco-Cola brand name. He helped found the concept of brand recognition through the use of coolers, pin-up girls, and the red and white signs still identifiable worldwide today.

Tin collectors normally specialize in one brand or type of product: Ex. Hershey, tea caddies, or one time period, 1840-1890.

Terminology:
- Biscuit tin: Normally associated with England, they were designed to hold biscuits (cookies), and are some of the most beautiful tins ever produced. They can demand high prices into the thousands of dollars.
- Miniatures: Also called sample tins, they held a trial amount of product for customers to try.
- Flat pocket: Tins made with hinged or lift off lids and small enough to slip into a pocket; very popular for tobacco products.
- Upright pocket: Tins with lift off lids.
- Store bins: Large storage bins supplied by the producer to country stores. The proprietor would scoop out the customer's requested amount.

Expensive to collect as very few survived the decline of the small town general store.
- Story tins: Adorned with characters that appealed to young children such as story-book characters.

Several factors affect the price paid for promotional material:
- The product advertised: Coke items resurged in popularity and created a mass influx of reproductions in the 1970s. Collectibles run from glass bottles, trays, right up to vending machines.
- The person or object shown in the ad: Can you walk into a retro restaurant without seeing Marilyn Monroe, Elvis, Humphrey Bogart, or James Dean?
- The Illustrator: Artist such as Norman Rockwell made their names famous as illustrators. Saturday Evening Post and Norman Rockwell were a team.
- When it was made: Antiques are a 100 years old, however, collectibles from the 1950s are big sellers. Demand determines value.
- Condition: Reproductions are a lighter weight tin and have paint that flakes. Refrain from purchasing the scratched or rusted tins. Check and make sure the top of the tin is the original.

Care:
If they need to be cleaned use a mild soap and soft cloth to dry.

Let them sit 24 hours without the lid to prevent rusting.

Keep them out of direct sunlight.

More on advertising in the following section.

Trivia: Gail Borden, born in 1801 in Norwich, New York, moved west to find a healthy climate for his persistent hacking cough. After a period in Kentucky, he moved to Mississippi where he was a well known surveyor and school teacher. His brother convinced him to move to Texas to pursue cattle ranching just in time for the war of independence with Mexico. He is credited with plotting the towns of Houston and Galveston. During the conflict Borden and his brother became the publishers of the *Telegraph* and *Texas Register*. Always a man of God, Borden wondered what he could do to preserve food and make it available to the thousands of children he had witnessed go hungry. With the loss of his wife and one son during a yellow fever epidemic, he became obsessed with refining food with a condensation method of preserving that he had invented. Meat was the first product he condensed and canned. California gold rush diggers and Artic explorers ate his meat pemmican biscuits. Still the public did not clamor for his product. On his way back to America from attending the 1852 London World's Fair, where he won a gold medal for his meat biscuit, Borden watched as young babies on the boat died from receiving milk from an infected cow. Borden vowed to find a way to condense milk. In 1856 he received a patent for his product that removed 80% of the water from milk, included sugar for preserving and to prevent discoloration, and a new copper vacuum pan and heating process that kept out air and reduced milk borne germs. His condensed milk was credited with lowering the infant mortality rate, which was his original goal. His Connecticut plant was still in financial difficulty until the outbreak of the Civil War. The army needed milk for its soldiers. They issued him a contract that established the company and its product, Borden's Eagle Brand Condensed Milk.

It Pays to Advertise—Part II

Walk in wisdom toward them that are without, redeeming the time. Let your speech be always with grace, seasoned with salt, that ye may know how ye ought to answer each man.   Colossians 4:4-5

    "Faster than a speeding bullet. More powerful than a locomotive. Able to leap tall buildings in a single bound. Yes, it's Superman." The lead-in stopped for a commercial message. Clark Kent and Jimmy Olsen sat down to a breakfast of Kellogg's Corn Flakes. And so did I and millions of other kids. I ate my Cherrios with my Lone Ranger deputy badge on.

    On Saturday mornings my dad took all of the Roy Rogers, Hopalong Cassidy, Gene Autry, and Sky King that he could stand, then he walked over and turned the channel to golf. Golf was all it took to get me outside. I'd dart across the street and lope around the school playground slapping my hip like I was riding Trigger.

    Dad knew when I'd enough of "the tube." We did our homework before we turned on our kid shows. Time Magazine, National Geographic, and Saturday Evening Post were around to keep us informed on world events. My parents made sure we grew up well-rounded.

Please lead families back to molding young minds. Help us not to use television to baby-sit, unmindful or ignoring the content of the program. Help us find another way to fill their time with constructive information.

    We junior rangers, deputy sheriffs, or G men learned life morality lessons in 30-minute episodes on a twelve inch, black and white screen Motorola. Television launched a new generation of consumers.

    Moving so often, my favorite advertisement promotion helped us pass the time in the car. I may not have been able to read, but I knew when to say "Burma Shave."

    In 1925 the owner's son, Allan Odell, came up with the idea of five or six consecutive signs with a catchy saying. Armed with $200 the young entrepreneur painted red signs with white letters and placed them along the highways of his native Minnesota. Speed limits were slower along the two lane highway system so it allowed the reader time to take in the verse. In the 1950s and 60s jingles eased the boredom. I loved "Substitutes / Can let you down / Quicker / Than a / Strapless gown / Burma Shave" or "Slow down Pa/Sakes alive / Ma missed signs / Four / And five / Burma Shave. They also reflected the decade, "We've made / Grandpa / Look so trim / The local / Draft board's after him / Burma Shave." Interstate highway speeds and the Highway Beautification Act of 1965 changed roadside promotions and ended the campaign.

You only have to view one episode of the History Channel's American Pickers to know signs are big sellers. Enamel sign collectors are put into two categories; country store and automotive.

Country store encompasses advertisements for food related or products that would have been purchased at a small town country store.

The popularity of NASCAR has further stoked the automotive/petrol collector formerly the home of the classic car collector. Anything having to do with the automotive industry has a market.

Early signs were labor intensive. Like tins, they were rolled iron, later they were made from rolled steel, and then tin-plated. Backgrounds, verbiage, and graphics were hand painted. Layers of color were applied, dried, and reapplied. In the late nineteenth century porcelain signs emerged. Artisans from Britain and Germany immigrated to provide a jump start for the fledgling American industry. Eventually, stenciling and silk screening techniques replaced the hand painted products. While thousands of signs were produced from 1900 to 1940, many were lost to the war industry during WWII. Scrap metal drives for the war effort were common.

Considered a 20th century phenomenon, the advertising character added a new dimension. Also aimed at the non-reader, these characters found on product labels were associated with the trademark. The Campbell Kids drawn by Grace G. Drayton adorned the walls of streetcars in 1906. Updated in 1951, they came out of retirement to entertain a new generation on television.

Nothing altered the habits of Americans like the automobile. The Duryea brothers of Springfield, Massachusetts redirected their focus from building bicycles to gasoline engine powered wagons. They incorporated Duryea Motor Wagon Company and sold the first American built automobile in 1896. Ransome Eli Olds moved from Lansing, Michigan to Detroit and opened the first assembly line factory in 1899. Here he moved from steam powered engines to gasoline engines. In 1913 Henry Ford moved from number three to the best selling company in the world after he installed a conveyor-belt assembly in his Highland Park, Michigan plant. His crews could fully assemble a new Model T in ninety-three minutes.

Before they were mass produced the few people lucky enough to need gas for a car would go to their local farm or hardware store and buy it by the can. The first filling station opened in St. Louis, Missouri in 1905. Just in time for the crush to own cars, the 1913 invention of the visible-cylinder resulted in a modern filling station being opened in Pittsburgh, Pennsylvania. Besides gas, car owners needed oil, tires, and service. A vast new industry arrived.

What collectors want:
- Graphics – The more color the better.
- Unusual shapes.
- Brand recognition.
- Condition – No bullet holes unless you can prove Dillinger shot it.
- Rarity.

Terminology:
- Advertising mirrors: Mirrored signs containing the name of a company and logo; lots of gold lettering is preferred. Originals are heavy, as the glass was a quarter inch thick.
- Calendars: Go back to the early days of advertising. They were a favorite of national and locals companies. Made of paper, many have been lost to age.
- Cigarette card: Also called a silk cigarette card, were trade cards used by tobacco companies to stiffen their packs and interest their customers. Produced first in 1875, early versions showed beautiful women, historical figures, Indians, and athletes.

- Counter display: A sign that sits on the counter. This sign is regarded as a point-of-sale advertisement.
- Crazing: A type of wear produced by environmental elements; aging or weathering are examples.
- Die cut: A non-standard produced sign. It's not round, rectangular, or square. They may be cut out or stamped, and had flaps that allowed them to stand.
- Fantasy sign: Verbiage taken from TV or movies such as Star Wars and Star Trek.
- Festoon: A non-metal, paper or cardboard sign that is hung over a drink fountain.
- Flange sign: A sign affixed so that it can be read from both sides.
- Menu board: A product sign that also contains an area where notes can be posted. Restaurants used these to announce their daily specials.
- Mirrors: Etched, gilded, or embossed, the mirror was a privileged 19th Century item.
- Neon: Illuminated tubes of colored neon gas formed to spell out company names or objects. Popular in the 1920s and 1930s.
- NOS – New old stock. Out of production, discontinued, or sat on a shelf and never sold. Many classic auto parts are NOS.
- Porcelain enamel: Powered glass called frit that is baked onto a metal or glass surface. The surface is weatherproof. These signs retain their vibrant color for long periods of time. Highly sought after by sign collectors.
- Push plate: A sign placed on or as the door handle. It's the first and the last thing a customer sees as he enters or exits an establishment.
- Reverse glass: The image is painted on the back of the glass.
- Self-framed: Signs that appear to have a frame around them.
- Showcards: Made of paper or poster board they were usually an off size Ex. Upcoming movie event signs.

- Standee: An easel back sign that can stand by itself. .Ex. Life-size cutouts of celebrities.
- Street car (Trolley Card): Mainly trolley, bus, or subway signs designed to fit into brackets mounted above the vehicle's windows. Standard size was 11" x 20.5".
- Swankyswigs: Free drinking glasses packed with a vendor's product. Kraft Cheese started the giveaway in the early 1930s. Jams and jellies followed until they were discontinued in the 1970s.
- Trays: Serving trays exist as the finest example of lithographed art. They have been extensively reproduced.

Trivia: Distributed by tobacco industry in 1886, the first baseball cards were black and white and contained in packs of cigarettes as promotions. In 1909 American Tobacco included color lithographed images of ball players in their packs as a marketing campaign. The T206 series of trade cards measured 1.5" x 2.5". Amongst the images were the famous ball players like Ty Cobb and Christy Mathewson, and a little known Pittsburg Pirate named Honus Wagner. Johannes Peter "Honus" Wagner, a non-tobacco user, sued American Tobacco for using his picture without his consent. He did not want his likeness to be part of a program to entice kids to smoke. Wagner won. His cards were recalled, but 57 were not recovered making them highly collectable. In February of 2007, one of Wagner's cards sold for $2.5 million at auction. "The T206 Honus Wagner card has long been recognized as the most iconic, highly coveted and valuable object in the field of sport memorabilia," said Dan Imler, managing editor of SCP Auctions. " Its legacy has transcended popular culture."

Honus Wagner was one of the first five men voted into the Baseball Hall of Fame in 1936.

A Stitch in Time

Wisdom is better than rubies; and all things that may be desired are not to be compared to it.   Proverbs 8:11

When my sister and I were tweens, Mom bought us each an embroidery hoop, embroidery needles, several colors of floss, and our first needlework projects. Pillow cases and tea towels awaited our creative endeavors.

Mom heated the iron and pressed the transfer on the clean white cotton surface. Light purple lines formed to make flowing floral baskets full of a variety of flowers. My little hands separated a long piece of floss until I had two strands. I put the ends in my mouth to make them wet and flattened them with my teeth. Now, the hard part; one hand held the needle as the second hand attempted to put the thread through the eye. Certainly the same brain, mine, was controlling both hands, although the multiple near misses made it seem unlikely. Finally, the large eyed needle accepted the thread. I pulled it through, knotted one end, and was ready to embroider a masterpiece worth presenting to a museum.

The back stitch was first. It seemed easy until Mom removed several hours of work and made me do it again; again; and finally again. The second stitch, the French knot, came easier. However, I soon learned that if you pull the thread too tightly to anchor the knot, it will come undone leaving you with one flat stitch. Needless to say, Mom removed the stitches and I did them again, and again. Finally, only the satin stitch remained. The secret to filling in the purple lines evenly evaded me for some days. Occasionally, a pricked a finger followed by a tiny spot of blood appeared. I quickly stuck the finger in my mouth so it wouldn't stain my towel and headed for the medicine cabinet and the stinging orange-red mercurochrome. A little blood seemed a small sacrifice for art. Once armed with my trio of stitches I was ready.

Hours were spent quietly sitting, moving my needle through and over, up and down. Maybe my being quiet was Mom's real goal, not my ability to craft works of art. No one ever asked me to frame one of my designs, but on Saturday mornings when ironing the pillow cases and tea towels, this young girl was very proud of her needlework.

Art is an expression of our inner being to be shared and enjoyed. It gives us a means to express our love for You, and the people and world around us. Lead us to be disciples and share our love with those who are looking for salvation.

You never know what you'll see at a flea market. Today, we checked out the First Monday Trade Days in Canon, Texas (www.firstmondaycanton.com). This really is a misnomer since the event runs the Thursday thru Sunday before the first Monday of a month. Since they have one hundred acres of vendors, you need three days and a Texas size wallet.

As I browsed, that means I'll look but I'm not ready to spend the limited amount of funds in my pocket, there on a vendor's table rested an old framed sampler. By its form and the theme of the piece it appeared to be the work of a young girl. It didn't look to have a name or date anywhere on the cross-stitched piece. Whoever framed it used a school group photograph from about the 1920s to stretch the linen and secure it in the old wooden frame. The sampler read, "Friends are lost by calling often and calling seldom."

It was the simplicity of the sampler that made me buy it. I could make up my own story of the little girl with needle in hand, sitting under a window or in a doorway to catch the natural light. Her stitches were meant to practice her alphabet and ciphers (numbers). She'd never know that her needlework would be appreciated by several future generations.

This type of needlework dates back to Egypt. The repetitive stitches functioned as a young girl's education in lettering, numbering, and memorizing intricate stitches. They also served as an artistic rendering of her life experiences. She may have spent her younger days in a day or boarding school or have been institutionalized in an orphanage. Middle class girls were already toiling in factories or laboring on family farms and had little time to devote to learning or needlework. The samplers were personal, and not thought of as something to collect until the 20th century.

Samplers belong to the category known as textiles. Whether the item is a woolen rug, quilt, or a silken sampler, textiles are fragile. Nature in the form of an insect, or man's need for cleanliness, results in fibers being eaten, worn out, or rotting.

Early American samplers date back to colonial times. Natural un-dyed brown linen with a weave count of 35, 36, or 40 was the fabric of choice for backgrounds. In today's market this count would be considered a "fine" material, such as used in t-shirts. Prosperous classes also utilized silk for backgrounds. Silk and metal threads were used.

The earliest creations were long and narrow leaving them unsuitable for framing. They are referred to as band samplers. The themes were numbers and alphabets, Biblical verses or scenes, and records of genealogy. Several stitches including the popular cross-stitch were applied. Motifs were suitable for clothing and household ornamentation. They may not be signed or dated. For this reason many colonial pieces may be accredited to England as they are English in design and workmanship. The strawberry and oak or acorn is contained in most early designs.

Later 1700s versions were square and included Adam and Eve, animals, especially the stag, and nature themes. Borders were added. Maps were introduced. Samplers were intended to be framed.

Those items from the Boston and Philadelphia schools are very desirable by collectors. The names found on those samplers often came from prominent families in American history. Teachers created the motifs of the samplers, not the student doing the needlework, making it easier to determine the region of the county where the young woman attended school.

At the end of the 19th century, rectangular shaped samplers were popular. Today collectors prefer pieces finished before 1850. During the 1850s needlework became a hobby and no longer the focus of a young lady's education. Quality became an issue as the hobbyist wasn't trained in one of the preeminent girl's schools. Inexpensive materials replaced the linen and silk. Coarser woven linen and wool thread took their place.

The determining factors of the value of samplers are:

- Age.
- Motif appeal.
- Condition.
- Region.

They range in price from the very inexpensive to six figure amounts. There are few reproductions.

Textiles are fragile and require special care:

Before touching, you should wash your hands to remove the natural skin oils.

Take off your jewelry to avoid catching a thread.

If mounting in a wooden frame use a sealed (such as a polyurethane varnish finish) frame and acid-free matting and backing.

Use UV-protected glass.

Do not display in direct sunlight or near heat sources.

When storing large pieces, roll and place in an acid free tube rather than folding. Put crumpled tissue paper in the free space in the tube.

If the item must be folded, refold every six months or the fabric will crease or breakdown in the folded areas.

Trivia: The oldest known American sampler is one created by Loara Standish, the only daughter of Captain Miles Standish, the military commander of the Pilgrims, and his wife, Barbara. On 50 count linen, the piece measures approximately 7¼" wide x 23½" tall. Done predominantly in blues and brown the motifs include the rose, carnation, oak leaf and an intertwined "S" above the verse. Circa 1640 to 1653, it is on display at the Pilgrims Hall Museum in Plymouth, Massachusetts, www.pilgrimhall.org.

It reads: "Loara Standish is my name/Lorde guide my hart that/I may doe thy will also/My hands with such/Convenient skill as may/Conduce to virtue void of/Shame and I will give/The glory to thy name."

Loara preceded her father in death. In his will he requested his sons bury him beside her.

Uncle Sam Needs You—Bob[3]

Yea, though I walk through the valley of the shadow of death, I will fear no evil: for thou art with me; thy rod and thy staff they comfort me. Psalm 23:4

There have always been men in our history that have responded when the country called. I can trace one branch back to the French and Indian Wars. Please indulge me as I tell you about three generations of my family.

Robert M. Thorn Sr., my grandfather, worked at a small dairy outside of Pittsburgh, Pennsylvania. Following the loss of civilian lives aboard the Lusitania, America joined the bloodbath known as World War I on the side of the Allied Powers. Granddad took a train to New York and enlisted in the Army. He thought the New York regiment would join the fight faster. He trained in communications. As a member of the Signal Corps, he was a carrier pigeon handler, he served in France.

In an earlier chapter I mentioned a cedar chest that had been lovingly packed with my grandmother's keepsakes. In that chest with her memorabilia was Granddad's World War I gas mask. None of my uncles and aunts wanted it so my dad gave it to me with some pictures and other odds-and-ends. Granddad had written across the back of his gas mask:

> "When I am in dire distress
> and with deadly gases prest
> Stick with me and save the day
> and we'll go back to the U.S.A."

When I read that it gave me a new insight into my granddad, the no-nonsense quiet man.

At the cessation of the "war to end all wars" in 1918, Granddad Thorn boarded the ship in France and returned home. He married and fathered seven sons and two daughters. At the time of Pearl Harbor his second oldest son and namesake, Robert M. Thorn Jr., had graduated from the Great Lakes Naval Station and was a young seaman.

Bob Jr., my dad, finished basic training and entered school for naval flight training. This would define the remainder of his life. During World War II he met and married my mom, who was serving in the Women's Army Corp as a Morse Code operator. He transferred to the Air Force when it was established as a separate branch of the military. After the war Dad left the Air Force, but he never lost the need to fly. He re-enlisted and retired after twenty-two years of service.

Robert M. Thorn III grew up knowing that service to our country flowed in his veins. As a teenager he joined the Pennsylvania Army Reserve. The Great Flood of 1977 in Johnstown, Pennsylvania saw this nineteen-year-old bagging bodies for two weeks. After training to be a helicopter mechanic, young Bob transferred to the Air Force Reserve. When the American Marine peacekeepers barracks in Beirut were bombed by a suicide extremist in 1983, his crew from Dover Air Force Base ferried the bodies back.

Bob met his wife, Ellen, who was also a young reservist, at Dover Air Force Base. When Desert Storm started both were called and served. Bob 3rd is now retired from the Air Force Reserve and works with his son, Braxton, and other young men in the Civil Air Patrol. Braxton completed glider training this summer. He will continue the family tradition.

My own son, Bill, broke his leg at Army bootcamp. He could have begged off, but he faced the challenge and drug around a cast in the South Carolina heat and humidity to graduate with his class.

That's what Americans, men and women, do.

Thank you for providing those willing to make sacrifices in their lives for the good of us all. Only through our prayers and their efforts will we be able to remain free. Help me provide support for the soldiers who gave of themselves for me, past and present.

This summer I gave my grandfather's gas mask to my brother. He already had Dad's medals and uniform. Now, he has a wonderful display of the three Bob Thorns' service.

There are so many types of militaria items, and such a large group of collectors that entire shows are available to peruse.

Colonial weapons in America were mainly the .75 caliber English Brown Bess and the .69 caliber French muskets. They were both flintlocks. Stocks were made from English walnut. They were smooth bore guns with no rifling. Later the British and French furnished "trade guns" to the Indians based on the two previously mentioned weapons. Indians sawed the barrel to a shorter length to carry easily through the woods. The manufacturers adjusted and produced the shorter barrel. Stocks were made of walnut or maple. Trade guns were cheaper but not as accurate.

As described in his book *The Kentucky Rifle*, by Captain John G. W. Dillin, the American rifle was more than a weapon of choice: "From a flat bar of soft iron, hand forged into a gun barrel; laboriously bored and rifled with crude tools; fitted with a stock hewn from a maple tree in the neighboring forest; and supplied with a lock hammered to shape on the anvil; an unknown smith, in a shop long since silent, fashioned a rifle which changed the whole course of world history; made possible the settlement of a continent; and ultimately Freed our country of foreign domination."

Early German immigrants are often credited with producing the American longrifle from the German hunting rifle. They developed a rifled barrel that aided accuracy. Most notable are Andreas Albrecht, Martin Meylin, J. Beck, Frederick Sell, and Andrew Verner of Pennsylvania. The early gunsmith had to multitask also as a silversmith, wood carver, and metal worker. The stocks were made from maple and curly maple with the fittings being brass or silver. The carving and inlays were first religious then later patriotic themes. Their guns may be marked or unmarked.

The workingman's backwoods rifles were made by local gunsmiths from whatever wood was available, had iron fittings, no carving, and no silver inlays. As it wore out, parts were re-used to make a replacement gun.

Many re-enactment venues flourish making pre-1850 Americana both collectible and reproduced. Black powder guns, tomahawks, and animal powder horns can be found on internet auction sites. Make sure you are dealing with a qualified representative. There are some beautiful examples at:

www.waynepwatson.com.

Availability of items is a major factor making the Civil War, World War I, and World War II the prime focus of American collectors.

At the start of the war there were not enough weapons stored by either side to arm their soldier so many used their own guns. Arms dealers and manufactures worked to meet the demand.

Several factors should be taken into consideration when buying antique guns. Blue (for nickel) is the rust preventive treatment given to guns at time of manufacture. The amount of bluing left determines how much the gun was used and affects the value. A maker's name, date, and serial number are helpful to verify age. Documentation will be requested if the maker is not shown on the piece. Condition is a factor. And as always, do your research before buying.

Civil War pistol collectors seek out the 1860 Colt Army Revolver issued to cavalry officers. The most common rifle carried by a northern foot soldier was the .58 caliber 3-band barrel Model 1861 Springfield. Confederate soldiers carried a 3-band .577 caliber British 1853 Enfield. Both were a single shot muzzle loading rifle musket.

Northern officers were issued the Model 1850 Army Staff & Field Officer' Sword, but preferred the cavalry officer's saber.

Daguerreotypes of Civil War soldiers in full uniform remain sought-after. Many soldiers, towns, or states on both sides provided their own clothing in the early years of the war. This led to a confusing variety of uniforms until official colors were established by 1863. Buttons, epilates, and insignia showed rank and are desired by enthusiasts.

There are additional items from the 1860s ranging from medical devices, confederate money, photographs, etc., at reasonable prices to fill the needs of this generation of collectors. Discharges signed by Lincoln are highly sought after by both military and autograph collectors. Newspapers were printed on highly acidic paper which left them fragile. Copies might be found on film in libraries or state historical societies.

International internet sites display products back to the Napoleonic wars; however the majority of objects are of the 20th Century: World War I, World War II, and the Cold War eras.

The Great War of 1914 through 1918, Americans refer to it as World War I, saw thousands of young boys in their prime cross the ocean to fight on foreign soil. When they came home, many carried back "war souvenirs" with them. Helmets, flags, swords and bayonets, and revolvers found their way into the doughboy's blue denim barracks bag. Their sons, who fought in World War II, brought back many of the same articles in their olive drab (OD) canvas duffel bags.

The majority of objects found on the Internet for sale are German. Whether German, Japanese, or Russian, be well read on what to expect. Buy a translation guide. Visit museums. Warman's also has books available for World War II collectors. Educate yourself.

Trivia: In 1907 Luger, a German company, constructed three prototypes of a .45-caliber 9-millimeter sidearm they wanted to sell to the American military. The U.S. Military declined. One of the prototypes is thought to have been destroyed. One is in a Louisiana museum. An anonymous gentleman bought the third in 1945 for $150. Sidney Aberman purchased the gun in 1949 for the same amount. Upon his death it was acquired by a California dealer who sold it to Yani Haryanto, an Indonesian billionaire, for $1 million. It has since traded hands several times. Last year the gun sold at public auction for a measly $430,000. The auctioneer congratulated the winner on his "great bargain" and said the sidearm will always be known as the "million dollar Luger."

Bibliography

Bellis, Mary.
   inventors.about.com/library/weekly/aacarsassemblya.htm

Berry, Letha.
   www.worthpoint.com/blog-entry/goodyear-rubber-head-dolls

Brunner, Michael.
   www.collectorsweekly.com/articles/an-interview-with-porcelain-advertising-sign-collector-michael-bruner

Clark, Hyla M. *The Tin Can Book.* New York, New York: The New American Library, 1977.

Costello, Robert B., ed. *American Heritage College Dictionary, 3rd Edition.* Boston, Massachusetts: Houghton Mifflin Company, 1993.

Cummings, Patricia. www.quiltersmuse.com/Samplers.htm

Fanning, Leonard M. Gail Borden, Father of the Modern Dairy Industry. www.diversifiedfoods.com/retail/borden/

Flayderman, Norm. *Guide to Antique American Firearms and Their Values. 9th Edition.* Iola, Wisconsin: Gun Digest Books, 2007.

Guns & Ammo website
   archives.gunsandammo.com/content/million-dollar-luger-goes-auction-block

Haskew, Michael E. *Warman's World War II, Collectibles: Identification and Price Guide 2nd Edition.* Iola, Wisconsin: Krause Publications, 2010.

Herlocher, Dawn. *200 Years of Dolls: Identification and Price Guide 4th Edition.* Iola, Wisconsin: Krause Publications, 2009.

"Cigarette Card" From Wikipedia, the free encyclopedia
   en.wikipedia.org/wiki/Cigarette_card

Crazy for Barbie
   www.crazyforbarbie.com

Goodyear Corporate Website.
   www.goodyear.com/corporate/history/history_story.html

NX Surplus website:
   www.nxsurplus.com/backpacks/duffle/history-of-military-duffle-bags

Squidoo website:
   www.squidoo.com/collectingvintageandantiquesigns

Huber, Carol. The ABC's of Sampler Collecting.
   www.AntiqueSamplers.com

Kovel, Ralph, and Terry. *Kovel's Antiques and Collectibles, 31st Edition, 1999 Price List*, New York, New York, Three Rivers Press, Crown Publishers, 1999.
LaChiusa, Chuck. Buffalo Architecture and History
www.buffaloah.com
Moran, Mark F. ed. 2010, Warman's Antique and Collectibles 2011 Price Guide, 44th Edition, Iola, Wisconsin, Krause Publications.
Ni, Ching-Ching.
articles.latimes.com/2010/mar/15/local/la-me-luger15-2010mar15
Ni, Ching-Ching.
inaminuteago.com/articles/samplerhist.html
Pristant, Carol. Antiques Roadshow 20th Century Collectibles, New York, New York, Workman Publishing Company Inc., 2003.
Renshaw, Alex.
webuy.advertisingantiques.co.uk
Rinker, Harry L. ed. Warman's Antiques and Collectibles, 5th Edition. Radnor, Pennsylvania: Wallace-Homestead Book Company, 1991.
Rooks, Bill.
www.palongrifles.com
Rosenberg, Jennifer. About.com.
history1900s.about.com/od/worldwari/p/World-War-I.htm
Schroy, Ellen T. ed. Warman's Antiques and Collectibles, 33rd Edition. Iola, Wisconsin: Krause Publications, 1999
Van Patten, Denise.
collectdolls.about.com.
Ward, Susan and Christopher Pearce, American Antiques and Collectibles. Edison, New Jersey: Chartwell Books, 1996.
Watson, Wayne.
www.waynepwatson.com
Pilgrim Hall Museum website.
www.pilgrimhall.org
Zoglin, Ron and Shouse, Deborah. Antiquing for Dummies. Foster City, California: IDG Books Worldwide, Inc., 1999.

CPSIA information can be obtained at www.ICGtesting.com
Printed in the USA
LVOW090958230712

291150LV00001B/27/P